Dancing in My Underwear

The Soundtrack of My Life

By Mike Morsch

Copyright© 2012 Mike Morsch

To Peter:

Always write!

Mike Morsch

9/10/12

With love for Judy, Kiley, Lexi, Kaitie and Kevin. And for Mom and Dad. Thanks for introducing me to some great music.

Published by
The Educational Publisher
www.EduPublisher.com

ISBN: 978-1-62249-005-9

Contents

Foreword
By Frank D. Quattrone
1

Chapters:
The Association
Larry Ramos
Dancing in my underwear
3

The Monkees
Micky Dolenz
The freakiest cool "Purple Haze"
9

The Lawrence Welk Show
Ken Delo
The secret family chip dip
17

Olivia Newton-John
Girls are for more than pelting with apples
25

Cheech and Chong
Tommy Chong
The Eighth-Grade Stupid Shit Hall of Fame
33

The Doobie Brothers
Tom Johnston
Rush the stage and risk breaking a hip?
41

America
Dewey Bunnell
Wardrobe malfunction: Right guy, right spot, right time
45

Three Dog Night
Chuck Negron
Elvis sideburns and a puka shell necklace
51

The Beach Boys
Mike Love
Washing one's hair in a toilet with Comet in the middle of Nowhere, Minnesota
55

Hawaii Five-O
Al Harrington
Learning the proper way to stretch a single into a double
61

KISS
Paul Stanley
Pinball wizard in a Mark Twain town
71

The Beach Boys
Bruce Johnston
Face down in the fields of dreams
79

Roy Clark
Grinnin' with the ole picker and grinner
85

The Boston Pops
Keith Lockhart
They sound just like the movie
93

The Beach Boys
Brian Wilson
Little one who made my heart come all undone
101

The Bellamy Brothers
Howard Bellamy
I could be perquaded
127

The Beach Boys
Al Jardine
The right shirt at the wrong time
135

Law & Order
Jill Hennessy
I didn't know she could sing
143

Barry Manilow
I right the wrongs, I right the wrongs
151

A Bronx Tale
Chazz Palminteri
How lucky can one guy be?
159

Hall & Oates
Daryl Hall
The smile that lives forever
167

Wynonna Judd
I'm smelling good for you and not her
173

The Beach Boys
Jeffrey Foskett
*McGuinn and McGuire couldn't get no higher . . .
and neither could I*
179

Hall & Oates
John Oates
Along with Yosemite Sam, the go-to guy for lip hair
187

Dan May
My album debut . . . sort of
193

The Lovin' Spoonful
Joe Butler
I believe in backstage magic
199

The Four Seasons
Bob Gaudio
Hey, get your hind end out of my ear, pal!
203

Epilogue
Elton John
I guess that's why they call it the blues
211

Acknowledgements
219

Dancing in My Underwear

Foreword
By Frank D. Quattrone

From the long, wide Leeway at Pekin (Illinois) Community High, the social epicenter of the teeming school, where many teenage plots were hatched, to the outfield grass at Iowa State University, where a baseball career came undone, from Mrs. Betty Bower's inspiring journalism class at Pekin High School to the bustling newsroom of the Cardunal Free Press in Carpentersville, Illinois, you're about to enter a terrain both alien and familiar.

In this joyous, reflective and sometimes flat-out funny memoir, longtime journalist and newspaper editor Mike Morsch presents us with the soundtrack of his life. And music — from the preternaturally sweet harmonies of the Beach Boys' "The Little Girl I Once Knew" to the social criticism of singer-songwriter Dan May's ironic "Paradise" — remains at the core of Mike's story.

You'll recognize the familiar teenage angst suffered by this good-natured, self-effacing lunk, even as you learn about growing up in the Sixties in the small-town simplicity of the Midwest. Along the way you'll come to enjoy the innocent adventures of Midwestern schoolboys, share in the home runs and strikeouts our young hero experienced on the baseball field (as well as his gaffes playing the field) and gain some insight into the once-golden years of the newspaper game.

But through it all, the turntable never stops spinning, the jukebox continues to jump and the songs never stop coming. Mike may have begun his distinguished career as a music lover by dancing in his underwear to the beats of the Beatles, Elvis and the Beach Boys in his parents' modest home, but now — as the executive editor of Montgomery Media, a group of multi-award-winning community online and print publications in Montgomery

1

Dancing in My Underwear

County, Pennsylvania (he's earned quite a few of them himself!) — Mike
has finally gotten the opportunity he never thought possible in his youth.

As a frequent contributor to Ticket, the weekly arts-and-entertainment
section of Montgomery Media, Mike has gotten to interview, meet and trade
quips [or stories] with some of the finest musical performers of this or any
other era.

Despite the preponderance of rock and pop artists — think Brian Wilson of
the Beach Boys, Micky Dolenz of the Monkees, Tom Johnston of the
Doobie Brothers, Daryl Hall and John Oates, and Chuck Negron of Three
Dog Night — you'll also be with Mike as he interviews stalwarts in country
(Wynonna and Roy Clark), classical (Keith Lockhart), and your
grandparents' music (Ken Delo of *The Lawrence Welk Show*).

And you'll find music connections in the most unexpected sources and
fields of interest — like art (KISS frontman Paul Stanley), comedy (Tommy
Chong from Cheech & Chong), TV (*Law & Order*'s Jill Hennessy) and
theater (*A Bronx Tale*'s Chazz Palminteri).

At the heart of it all, Mike shares with you some of the insights he's gleaned
from interviews with these paragons of modern music. You'll hear it in their
own voices. Meanwhile, you'll come to know a most engaging character in
his own right — a man who grows before your eyes from a certified
member of "The Eighth-Grade Stupid Shit Hall of Fame" to a loving father
and a highly respected member of his profession.

So sit back, fire up the turntable or click on your iPod and let Mike take you
on an unforgettable journey through the soundtrack of his life.

The Association
Larry Ramos
Dancing in my underwear

My folks, Ed and Ann Morsch, had quite a record collection when I was a kid in the 1960s. Much of that music would now be considered hip for its time — the Beatles, the Beach Boys and Elvis — the biggest popular music stars of that era. Mostly, though, my folks favored music that featured harmonies.

I think it was because they shared a fondness for the local barbershop chorus in our town. They had a friend, Jim, who was one of the singers and they often attended the local concerts. The local guys had cut a couple of albums – I guess they were that good – and it was at those concerts where my folks purchased those barbershop albums.

Around the age of 4, I discovered my parents' record collection, which consisted of both albums and 45s, the smaller vinyl disks that had one song on each side of the record. There are actually photographs of the 4-year-old me dancing in my underwear next to that gray record player, eyes closed and completely oblivious to my parents taking pictures of what they considered was cute behavior by their eldest child.

Fortunately, the older I got, the more prone I was to wearing pants while dancing. But that took nothing away from the enthusiasm I've had for music along life's journey, pants or no pants.

The first 45 record I can recall playing on the small, gray record player that we had was "The Little Girl I Once Knew" by the Beach Boys. I was immediately attracted to the harmonies of brothers Brian, Dennis and Carl Wilson, their cousin Mike Love and high school friend Al Jardine. It would be the beginning of a lifetime of love for that sound and those lyrics and there was no way at such a young age I could have known how important the Beach Boys would be throughout my life.

In what seems odd now, though, there were no Beach Boys albums in the collection that I can recall. So the one album I gravitated toward because of that attraction to the harmonies was "Insight Out" by the Association. It featured two wonderful songs and big hits — "Windy," which reached No. 1 in 1967 and "Never My Love," which climbed to No. 2 that same year.

Not only was I attracted to the music, but also the album cover, which featured single-, double-, triple- and quadruple-exposed individual portraits of the band's members. Released in 1967, it was the first album by the group that featured Larry Ramos, a guitarist and vocalist who had replaced lead guitarist Jules Alexander.

I absolutely wore that album out. And more than 40 years later, I got to talk with Larry Ramos.

In July of 2011, three original members of the Association – Ramos, Russ Giguere and Jim Yester – joined the 2011 version of the "Happy Together Tour" for a July 13 show at the Keswick Theatre in Glenside, Pa.

Other '60s musical icons on the bill included the Turtles, featuring Flo and Eddie; the Grass Roots; Mark Lindsay, former lead singer for Paul Revere & the Raiders; and the Buckinghams.

"Here we are, grandfathers, but we're still having a great time, we're still kids," said Ramos in a telephone interview from his home in Idaho. "It's kinda far out. Jules [Jules Alexander, another original member of group that Ramos had replaced in the late 1960s, returned and then left again and no longer tours with the group] used to say, 'You know, this is a lot more fun as adults.' And he was absolutely right."

4

Although the Association had broken up and re-formed several times with different lineups over the past 40 years, this wasn't its first time on the Happy Together Tour. The band appeared in the 1984 Happy Together Tour, which also featured The Turtles, among others.

"We were very careful back then with the music we selected because we wanted the music to endure," said Ramos of the band's early years. "We didn't care about where the music came from as long as it was good.

"I think that's one of the reasons why we're still around. We were so careful in selecting the material that we recorded and the quality of the material that we recorded. 'Never My Love' is a classic. I love that song and I loved it the first time I ever heard it," said Ramos.

Still, Ramos said he and the other members enjoy performing more now than they did in the group's heyday.

"In the '60s, it was work, man. We were cranking out a couple of hundred days a year on the road," said Ramos. "Now, when we sing our love songs, the boomers are kids again. They hold each other's hands and sing along. It's very, very touching.

"The music is the whole thing. Certain things in music trigger those emotions. I'm so happy that our music has sustained the ability to do that and has become part of the fabric of American music," he said.

Ramos, who has been performing since the age of 5, described himself as "a Filipino kid from West Kauai, Hawaii." As a youngster who played the ukulele, he appeared in the 1950 film "Pagan Love Song," starring Esther Williams, Howard Keel and Rita Moreno. He eventually went on to perform with the New Christy Minstrels before joining the Association.

Dancing in My Underwear

And he's grateful to have been doing what he loves for as long as he's been doing it.

"I honestly didn't think my career would be this long," he said. "I only planned my life until I was 65. I'm a little past that now and I don't know what the heck I'm doing. I'm just enjoying it now. Being able to be in this business at this age, it's just terrific.

"Our music affected people in a way that's stayed with them all these years. That's probably the biggest reward that any recording artist or any entertainer can have."

I'm one of those people. The music of the Association has stayed with me all these years.

On the night of the concert, I was very excited. So many years had passed since I was a 4-year-old dancing in my underwear to the music of the Association on my small, gray record player.

The copy of "Insight Out" that my folks had was long gone, but I found another original copy of the album at a record store in Chestnut Hill, Pa., few weeks before the show. I was hoping to get a chance to meet the Association guys and have them sign my album.

Fortunately, I got to do just that. But it almost didn't happen.

I shared the Happy Together concert with my oldest daughter Kiley, which was lucky for me. She was riding shotgun during the autograph-getting portion after the show. She has seen me collect autographs her whole life and knows that I oftentimes get star-struck when in the presence of the artists. That experience makes her a perfect second in those situations, kind of a Vice President in Charge of Making Sure That Dad Doesn't Act Like a Babbling Teenager and Forget to Get the Autograph.

6

I had already secured the signatures of Giguere and Yester on the album cover when Ramos came out in front of the stage for the meet-and-greet. I was so excited to meet him that I forgot to ask him to sign the album. Like Ramos, I'm getting older, too, I guess.

"Dad, the album!" said Kiley, saving the day. Ramos signed the album cover, completing the Association autograph trifecta for me that evening.

My daughter, whose big-deal music group is N'SYNC, was familiar with only a few of the songs from the Happy Together show, which also included performances of classic songs like "Kind of a Drag" by the Buckinghams; "Midnight Confessions" by the Grass Roots; "Kicks" by Mark Lindsay of Paul Revere and the Raiders; and "Happy Together" by the Turtles.

In addition to meeting the guys from the Association, we also got to meet Carl Giammarese of the Buckinghams and Howard Kaylan of the Turtles and get their signatures.

When I introduced Kaylan to my daughter, he said, "You should thank your father for introducing you to good music."

With all due respect to N'SYNC, Kaylan is right. There was some great, great music in the 1960s. And Kiley and I enjoyed seeing all those talented musicians whose songs have stayed with me all these years.

You might say we were happy together.

The Monkees
Micky Dolenz
The freakiest cool "Purple Haze"

As the superintendent of Rankin Grade School, a little country school that sat between Pekin and South Pekin, Illinois with a total of about 120 students in grades kindergarten through eighth grade, my dad always seemed to want to do nice things for his students, especially the eighth-graders.

The eighth-graders always got to take a big field trip at the end of their last year at Rankin, most often to Six Flags south of St. Louis, which ended up being about a four-hour bus ride. It must have been a difficult trip with a bunch of young teenagers, mostly because those trips were made on the yellow school buses, not the fancy chartered buses of today, complete with restroom facilities.

I can remember as a little kid always wanting to go on that trip with my folks, hoping that time would hurry up and make me an eighth-grader. My parents often got home very late in the evening from that trip, and try as I might, I was never able to stay awake long enough to see what souvenir they would bring home for me.

One year, I got a boat oar – not a full-sized oar but a sawed-off souvenir one about half the size of a real oar – with the Six Flags logo on it. It was an odd-gift for an 8-year-old, considering the fact that we didn't own a boat and didn't live particularly close to any body of water that might comfortably accommodate a boat.

But in addition to the annual field trip, the 1968 eighth-grade class of Rankin Grade School got an extra-special gift from my folks as it neared graduation: a party in the basement of my parents' home.

Dancing in My Underwear

My dad, a stern disciplinarian at school that was probably typical of school administrators in the 1960s – it occurred to me later that the boat oar he brought home from Six Flags was about the perfect size for paddling unruly students – was in truth a kindhearted gentleman who always had the students' best interests in his heart, even though it could sometimes be a little sideways.

Hosting a party in his basement was one of those times, mostly because it was not a finished basement. Oh, our family used it like it was a finished basement – there were plenty of kids' toys strewn about, some furniture and a rug down there, along with a working fireplace. But there was no "family room" feel about it. The laundry area was just at the bottom of the steps and to the left, but it was a dark and damp area of uncarpeted cement floors and cinder block walls. In fact, there was an area toward the back of the basement that my folks used as a storage area that scared the beejeezus out of me. It was dark and damp and there wasn't a spider in the neighborhood that hadn't spun a web back there.

When it rained a lot, the water would virtually come through some of the compromised areas of the cinder blocks and flood the cement floor. A countless number of times my dad would have to get down there and spend hours vacuuming up the water. I assume that's why the basement was never finished – it leaked like a sieve.

But hey, it seemed like an OK location for an eighth-grade party to my dad. I don't recall much about that party – it's likely I wasn't invited downstairs for much of the festivities – but I do recall that a few of the eighth-grade boys had formed a garage band and they were the featured entertainment for the evening. Lucky for them and their amplifiers that it didn't rain that evening and they weren't standing in two inches of water with those electric guitars.

A kid by the name of Greg Clemons was the lead singer for that band and I was quite impressed with his version of the Monkees' hit tune "Last Train to Clarksville," which was the group's debut single and hit No. 1 on the Billboard charts in 1966. I was a big fan of the Monkees then, and I never missed their Saturday-morning television show and the antics and music of Micky Dolenz, Davy Jones, Peter Tork and Michael Naismith.

And in September of 2011, I got to talk with Micky Dolenz.
The first clue Dolenz got that the Monkees were a huge success could just have easily been a fire drill.

The Monkees – formed as a musical acting quartet in 1966 that served as America's answer to the Beatles — had been sequestered for months in the studio, engulfed in rehearsing, filming and recording.

In essence, they had no idea of the public reaction to "The Monkees" television show because they hadn't yet been out in public to experience it.

Just before Christmas of 1966, the band members got a week off. Dolenz decided to do a little Christmas shopping at his local mall in Los Angeles, where he grew up, with plans to head up to San Jose, California, after that to see his family for the holidays.

"I get out of my car and I have my list and I go through the big glass doors of the mall and all of a sudden I hear screaming and people are running toward me," said Dolenz in a telephone interview from Los Angeles. "And I thought it was a fire. So I turned around and I opened the glass doors and I go, 'This way! This way! Don't panic! Calm down! Walk slowly this way!'

"All of a sudden I realized there was no fire; it's all these people — mostly kids — running at me. So I ran back and got in my car and I was kind of pissed because I couldn't do my Christmas shopping. That was the first inkling I had of the success of 'The Monkees,'" he said.

11

Dancing in My Underwear

And 45 years later, Dolenz is still a success. I talked to him for a preview story about a solo gig he had planned at the 360 Club at the Parx Casino in Bensalem, Pennsylvania.

Dolenz — who along with Jones and Tork had been busy with a successful 45th anniversary tour for the Monkees before it was abruptly stopped a month earlier — had sprinkled a few solo gigs into his summer and early fall schedule.

There was no official reason given at the time for the stoppage of the tour which began in England in May 2011, reached the U.S. in June and had its plug pulled in early August.

Although he wouldn't comment further, Dolenz did say that the band was having fun during the tour.

"The shows were really great, some of the best we've ever done. It was very gratifying," he said.

The Monkees had a number of hits in the late 1960s, including "Last Train to Clarksville" (the group's first No. 1 in 1966); "I'm a Believer" (No. 1 in 1966); "Daydream Believer" (No. 1 in 1967); and "Pleasant Valley Sunday" (No. 3 in 1967). The group has reunited off and on over the years as a trio mostly without the participation of Nesmith.

Dolenz, then 66, has had a career that not only includes being a musician but also a stage actor, television director and radio personality. But there has always been the music.

"'The Monkees' was a television show, so we had little or no control over what was being recorded. I didn't have a big problem with it at the time in the early days because I'd take it as an assignment, more or less," said Dolenz, who by the time "The Monkees" gig rolled around had already starred in the television series "Circus Boy" in 1956.

"But you look at the songwriters who wrote those songs [for the Monkees] and it's unbelievable; it's a Who's Who of songwriting: Tommy Boyce and Bobby Hart, Neil Diamond, Carole King, Neil Sedaka, Harry Nilsson, Paul Williams . . . just amazing songwriters," he said.

In his solo act, Dolenz has always tried to make sure to give the fans what they came to hear — all those hits from the Monkees. He also said he's gotten better over the years at relating to his audience.

"In the early days, we couldn't relate to an audience because they were all just screaming," said Dolenz. "In the early days of my solo show, I would just stand there with a guitar and play and sing. But then I started doing a lot of musical theater and I got a lot better at being comfortable without an instrument in my hands."

Previously published reviews at the time indicated that Dolenz's voice remained strong, and he agrees.

"Most of that I attribute to the training that I've been doing for musical theater," said Dolenz, whose most recent stage work was a successful run of starring in "Hairspray" in London. "I warm up and train properly and keep my voice in shape."

And like most artists, Dolenz said he doesn't like the travel, but he still gets a kick out of performing.

"Like I tell people, they pay me to travel . . . I sing for free. I love doing these shows," he said.

Dolenz's show in September 2011 at the Parx Casino was scheduled for 5 p.m. on a Sunday, a somewhat odd day and start time for a concert by a big

star. But let me tell you about 5 p.m. Sunday concerts: They are, quit
simply . . . beautimous. Not only does the early evening start time fall afte
my Sunday afternoon nap, but I was home in time to have dinner with m:
family and well ahead of the Phillies game, which had an 8 p.m. start tim
that evening on ESPN.

And what else can one say about Micky Dolenz that hasn't already bee1
said? It was the music that kept me coming back to that show as a kid, an
it's the music that keeps me coming back more than 40 years later.

I had the pleasure of shaking hands with Dolenz at the meet-and-gree
before the performance Sunday evening. It's worth noting that he wear
really cool hats because I'd like to wear really cool hats, too. Unfortunately
I am unable to get clearance from the tower on that. When I told The Blond
Accountant that Dolenz was wearing a cool hat and that I should get on
too, she informed me that I wasn't Micky Dolenz and that I didn't have
resume filled with hit songs.

I was aware of that.

Although he'll always be remembered as one of the Monkees, Dolenz i
quite an accomplished singer and musician as well as a television an
theater actor and director, Saturday-morning cartoon voiceover performe
and radio personality.

The history of the Monkees is well documented, but I sometimes learn
thing or two during the between-song banter that a performer has with th
audience. In this instance, most of the new information for me came fron
the non-Monkees stories.

During the Parx show, Dolenz shared an anecdote about the great Jim
Hendrix. Because of Hendrix's performance at the 1967 Monterey Po:
Festival, Dolenz suggested to Monkees' management that Hendrix open fo

the group on its first American tour. Hendrix eventually did a few gigs with the Monkees.

Dolenz then performed his version of Hendrix's song "Purple Haze," which for me qualified as the freakiest cool moment of the show.

Another story that I enjoyed was Dolenz telling about the time he traveled to London and got to attend a recording session that the Beatles were having at the time. It was in the late 1960s and John, Paul, George and Ringo were working on their "Abbey Road" album. One of the tracks they played for Dolenz that day was "Oh! Darling," and Micky's rendition of the song followed his telling of that story.

And Dolenz's version of Chuck Berry's "Johnny B. Goode" was absolutely outstanding, mostly because he's been doing it for quite some time. In fact, Dolenz revealed that it's the song he sang during his audition for the Monkees, the one that essentially got him the job.

Of course, Dolenz was the lead singer on some of those great Monkees' hits like "Last Train to Clarksville," "I'm a Believer" and "Steppin' Stone," and all of those were included in the Sunday solo show, which also featured Dolenz's sister — Coco Dolenz — singing backup, which she does for his solo appearances.

Shifting into concert reviewer mode for a moment, I must say that Dolenz has still got some great pipes and maintains that theatrical presentation to his audiences. He offered the standing room-only crowd — one of the biggest if not the biggest for a show at Parx's 360 Club — a lot of energy along with a lot of memories.

Everybody seemed to go away happy, including me. It was a great show by a great performer and pop culture icon. Sure, the crowd was older — the Monkees' heyday was in the late 1960s — but I'm guessing I'm not the only

Dancing in My Underwear

one who was pleased with a 5 p.m. Sunday concert. We may not be able to dance the night away, but we old folks have got that toe-tapping thing down better than any other age group.

In fact, in this instance, you might say it was another Pleasant Valley Sunday.

The Lawrence Welk Show
Ken Delo
The secret family chip dip

From the Department of It's Hip to Be Square, more than 40 years later, I find that I enjoy watching reruns of the old "Lawrence Welk Show," now shown in the Philadelphia area Sunday evenings on PBS.

"You're not watching that again, are you?" The Blonde Accountant will say to me every time she walks into the family room and good old Lawrence is ah-one ana ah-twoing.

My parents are to blame for this. I can trace my affection for the show back to the regular television routine our family had when I was a kid, which included watching the Welk show.

You may begin making fun of me for being an old guy, because the show was and probably still is perceived as an old-people show. Old people liked watching it on television then and old people liked sitting in Lawrence's studio audience listening to that big band sound for many years from the 1960s to the 1980s.

When thinking back on it, though, my parents weren't old in the 1960s. My dad was in his mid- to late-30s and my mom, six years his junior, was right around 30. That's not old.

They probably liked the Welk show because they had grown up with their parents listening to big band music on the radio.

But I really disliked big band music in the late 1960s, probably like every other kid in America at the time. Even at 9 years old, I had already been exposed to the Beach Boys, the Beatles and Elvis, among others, and kudo⋮ to my folks for being cool young parents in that musical era.

But "The Lawrence Welk Show" turned out to be part of a family traditio⋮ in a simpler era that still evokes — as Mr. Welk might say — wunnerful wunnerful childhood memories. So I'm glad I was able to tolerate it enoug⋮ then to get to the sweet payoff from it now.

Saturday evenings were indeed a big deal in the Morsch household in th⋮ late 1960s. In addition to "The Lawrence Welk Show" — which my youn⋮ ears heard as "The Loren Swelk Show" — it was also oftentimes "Morsc⋮ dip" night. It was a real treat then as it is today.

How to explain the Morsch dip? Conventional thinking by those who knev⋮ our family might assume that the "Morsch dip" was just a nickname for ⋮ goofy relative, but such was not the case.

No, Morsch dip is a secret family recipe for potato chip dip, the mai⋮ ingredient being Philadelphia Cream Cheese. Who knew that if only I ha⋮ read the potato chip dip tea leaves correctly back then, they would hav⋮ provided clues as what would lie ahead for me on the East Coast?

(As an aside, it turns out The Blonde Accountant is not that fond of Morsc⋮ dip because she thinks it is too plain. It is. We were a bland family when ⋮ came to foods. According to her, though, it needs garlic, but that ingredie⋮ is not in the secret family recipe and Morsch dip would not be considere⋮ authentic with garlic in it.)

Once we kids got our bowl of chip dip in hand and parked ourselves on th⋮ floor in front of the TV, my younger sister and brother and I would b⋮ subjected to "The Lawrence Welk Show," which I'm sure elicited quite a b⋮ of whining from the three of us between the bites of chips and dip.

18

But parents bribing children with food to keep them quiet is an age-old tradition, and it seemed to work on us. Although I didn't think I was paying attention to "The Lawrence Welk Show" back then, I enjoy it quite a bit now. The musicians and their "champagne music" were top-rate, the singing and dancing was superb and, of course, it's always fun to see the hairstyles and fashions from that era.

The other thing about the Welk show was that, for whatever reason, I still remember the words to the theme song. Go figure.

Goodnight, goodnight, until we meet again
Adios, Au Revoir, Auf Wiedersehn 'til then
And though it's always sweet sorrow to part
You know you'll always remain in my heart
Goodnight, sleep tight, and pleasant dreams to you
Here's a wish and a prayer that every dream comes true
And now 'til we meet again
Adios, Au Revoir, Auf Wiedersehn
Goodnight!

Nearly 40 years later, I interviewed one of those performers, Ken Delo, whom I watched every week on the Welk show. Delo, a song-and-dance man – was a real showman, and even as a child, I recognized a sense of playfulness in his performances between bites of chips and dip.

"A lot of kids were forced into watching that show," said Delo in a January 2012 telephone interview from his home in Arizona. "Even today, a lot of women tell me, 'Oh ya, I used to watch that show on Saturday nights when I was doing my hair.'"

Delo had actually made a name for himself in the entertainment business well before he joined the Welk family. He and his partner, John Daly, had a Dean Martin and Jerry Lewis comedy-variety act that hit big in Australia in the early 1960s. "Delo and Daly" found steady work on Australian television and in nightclubs down under for much of the 1960s.

Dancing in My Underwear

But it wasn't steady enough for Delo. While in Australia, he met dancer and singer Arthur Duncan, who by the late 1960s had secured a spot as a regular on the Welk show. Duncan arranged for Delo to audition for Welk and the show's producer and Delo impressed Welk enough to be offered three guest spots on the show in the summer of 1969.

By that October, Delo was a regular on the show, joining Duncan and other regular cast performers that included Myron Floren, Bobby Burgess, Norma Zimmer, Dick Dale, the Lennon Sisters, Joe Feeney, Guy Hovis and Ralna English, Mary Lou Metzger, Ava Barber, Bob Ralston, Anacani and many others.

"I figured I'd give it a year and see what happens," said Delo. "First of all, it was a steady job. And because we were known from TV, we got a lot of bookings, too.

"People would say to me, 'Why do you want to be on 'The Lawrence Welk Show?' You know, we were getting paid every week. And we had some really good musicians," he said.

Delo remained with "The Lawrence Welk Show" until it ended its original run in 1982. And during that run, he accumulated a career full of great stories, which he still likes to tell.

Like the time he sang a song from the top of the ladder at Madison Square Garden in New York during one of the many tours that the Welk performers embarked upon.

"We played Madison Square Garden twice – we played all the biggest coliseums all over the country and just filled them. Lawrence was a real draw," said Delo.

During all those years of touring, Delo said he never would stay in his dressing room during the show. He'd stand backstage and watch because, as he put it, "I knew someday this was going to be over. And I got a chance to hear the greatest band that's ever been around."

In the larger venues, like Madison Square Garden, tickets were sold that offered a limited view of the performers, like from behind and above the stage. The performers would literally have their backs to that segment of the audience for the entire show.

"So I'm standing there watching the show and a guy comes down from way in the top and he has a note, and he said, "Mr. Delo, would you give this to Lawrence? We paid a lot of money for these tickets and we can't see the faces of the performers.' I said, 'I'll give it to him.'"

He noticed one of the stage hands standing over on the other side of the stage, so Delo approached the man.

"I went over to him and said, 'I'm coming on next. When I come onstage, if I do this – and I made a hand gesture – bring that ladder that is right there over to the side of the stage and let me pull it up onstage," said Delo.

When Welk introduced Delo to the Madison Square Garden audience, Delo handed him the note from the audience member. Delo then gave the stage hand the high sign, walked over and dragged the ladder onto the stage.

"Lawrence is looking at me like, 'What the heck is this?' I put the ladder right in the middle of the stage in front of the band. And I was going to do 'Rock-a-bye,' a little Al Jolson thing. I climbed up to the top of the ladder and faced only the people in back. And I sang the whole song up there," said Delo.

Dancing in My Underwear

"I said to Lawrence when I got up on the ladder, 'The people in back want to see our faces.' And then I cued them and the band went into my song. I sang the whole thing and when I finished I've never heard an ovation like that. I climbed down, grabbed the ladder and went offstage," said Delo.

The next day, at the next tour stop, Welk approached Delo before the show and said, 'Ken, can we do that ladder thing again?'

"I said, 'Lawrence, it doesn't work here. It's too low back there. It's not the same setup.' But those were the kind of things I got away with, so Lawrence just let me do it."

Live television Welk show performances also provided Delo with memorable moments. Like the time he was scheduled to sing the song "I'm an Old Cowhand."

"To this day, people keep saying that it was set up, but it wasn't," said Delo. In that bit, Delo was dressed as a cowboy, complete with a big yellow hat and red chaps, which according to Delo was a costume that Bob Hope had worn in one of his movies.

"Bobby [Burgess] and Cissy [King] were sitting on the stairs. All of our cast members were on the stage. I finished the first chorus singing to Mary Lou [Metzger], and I walked over to where Cissy and Bobby were. And I don't know what made me say this, but I said, 'Now you pay attention, girl!" One second after I said that, my chaps fell off. And the cast members went nuts on the stage. It looked like my pants fell off," said Delo.

So he sang the whole thing, trying to stifle his laughter, which forced him to make up some of the lyrics. At the end of the song, he took the costume six guns and faux-fired them into the air – which appeared real, thanks to a good sound man – and then walked off the stage, chaps dragging around his ankles.

"The camera then cut to Lawrence over by the audience. He usually didn't ad-lib anything, and he said, 'Ken, let's keep the show clean.'"

Lawrence Welk died on May 17, 1992, at the age of 89, and his funeral provided Delo with one final touching and special moment.

"At the Hollywood Cemetery, we were all there in this chapel. And some of the guys played Dixieland, because that was his favorite music," said Delo.

"Then we all went out to the gravesite and the casket was going to be lowered into the ground. So all of us are standing around, and the Lennon Sisters were right behind me. And all of a sudden, without anybody planning it, we all started singing the 'Goodnight' song. I thought, 'Am I going to get through this without crying?' Everyone was all choked up," he said.

Talking to Ken Delo was a real treat. It took me back to those days when I was a kid in my parents' living room, being forced to watch "The Lawrence Welk Show" but thinking that it might be an acceptable tradeoff because of the special treat of Morsch dip.

Now, I still watch the reruns of those old shows, and every once in a while, I'll make myself some Morsch dip as a treat.

As Mr. Welk might say, it's all still so very wunnerful, wunnerful.

Olivia Newton-John
Girls are for more than pelting with apples

In the mid-1960s, my folks moved from a small house with a small yard at 1417 North 12th St. in Pekin to a bigger home with a large yard at 52 S. Deveron Circle in a new development of approximately 70 houses a few miles south of town called Glorianne Acres.

It's fair to say that many people not from Pekin considered it to be a rural redneck area. So moving south of Pekin just outside was really living out in the sticks. There was actually an even smaller town farther south called, appropriately enough, South Pekin. It was actually where my dad was born and raised, so to him, the move to Glorianne Acres was "moving into town."

Our neighborhood was laid out in an oval, with houses on both the inside and outside of the oval. There was only one entrance into the development off 14th Street, across a small bridge over a small creek. Kids from the neighborhood used to congregate at "the bridge" and just hang out. In fact, I learned the basic facts about the birds and bees from some of the older teenage guys in the neighborhood while killing time hanging out at "the bridge." I didn't learn until later on that those know-it-all jamokes didn't have all their facts straight about the birds and the bees.

Our brick ranch house had plenty of yard, enough in fact to have our own personal baseball field in the backyard. The back of the house served as the leftfield wall, our back yard swing set was the centerfield fence and the clothesline several feet beyond the swing set was the centerfield upper deck. In right field, any ball hit on a fly that cleared the neighbor's property line was considered a home run.

Our garden ran the length of our lot, from behind home plate all the way down the rightfield line. But because my folks didn't exactly have a green thumb, lost baseballs were probably the most plentiful vegetable in the garden.

Looking from the street, the neighbors to our north had a similar brick ranch house and almost exactly the same-sized lot. The summer before my eighth grade year in 1974, the Cook family moved in next door, and they had two boys, one of whom was my age and going into eighth grade as well.

Rick Cook was a big kid for his age. A quiet and unassuming guy, he didn't say a whole lot, but he was as smart as a whip. He joined the neighborhood crew of eighth-grade knuckleheads that included Bob Bearden, Randy Hodgson and me. Rick gave our little group a bit of credibility in the brain department, which actually wasn't saying much for us. Our idea of a good time before Rick moved into the neighborhood was hanging out in the apple orchard at the north end of the development and trying to impress the neighborhood girls by throwing apples at their heads. It's pretty safe to say that none of us had yet figured out the finer points of wooing the women.

When we weren't playing baseball, walking in the creek or on the railroad tracks just west of the development or hanging out at the bridge, we would just ride our bicycles around the development's oval.

Rick had other ideas, something along the lines that challenged us to think a little bit, surely a foreign concept to me at that age: He wanted to play board games in his basement, more specifically the board game Risk.

Risk is a turn-based game that can have up to six players. But Rick and I always played two-handed because every time he suggested we play the game, Bob and Randy conveniently disappeared.

The Risk board was a political map of the Earth, divided into 42 territories on six continents. The object of the game was to occupy every territory and eliminate me, which Rick had no trouble doing to the tune of about 100 times during the summer before eighth grade.

In the end, it was worth getting my brains knocked out by Rick at Risk because he redeemed himself that summer by introducing me to the music of Olivia Newton-John.

The album was the 1974 release "If You Love Me Let Me Know," which produced two hits for Olivia Newton-John, the title track and "I Honestly Love You," which became her first No. 1 hit.

But as much as I liked those songs, it was the album cover of "If You Love Me Let Me Know" that impressed me more. Olivia was absolutely stunning on that album cover to the not yet 14-year-old me. It was the first time that I realized that maybe girls were more than just targets for my apple throwing.

By the time 1978 rolled around and the film "Grease" was released, I was well past the apple-throwing stage with girls and very well aware of why John Travolta was singing "You're the One That I Want" after he saw Olivia Newton-John in those tight black pants.

And more than 30 years later, I picked up the telephone in my office to hear, "Mike, this is Olivia Newton-John."

It was all I could do not to go all Travolta on her and respond, "Sandy?"

Newton-John was going to be in West Chester, Pa., in March 2010 to headline a two-day event that focused on health, wellness and environmental conservation called "Olivia: Voices For Healing . . . Our Planet . . . Ourselves" at West Chester University.

The event was a benefit for the ACEER Foundation (Amazon Center for Environmental Education and Research), the College of Health Sciences

27

Dancing in My Underwear

Annual Integrative Health Conference and Masters of Public Health (MPH) with Integrative Health Track and the Olivia Newton-John Cancer and Wellness Centre Appeal.

"I'm not an expert, I'm not a cancer doctor. I'm just a woman who has been through the experience and here I am 18 years later and I'm OK," said Newton-John in the telephone interview from her home in West Palm Beach, Fla. "As women, I think we tend to not take care of ourselves because we put everybody else first. So I have little pointers for women in that area of things they can do to make sure they do that."

Newton-John gave the keynote address with co-presenter Dr. Jonathan Cebon, director of oncology at Austin Health in Melbourne, Australia, at West Chester University's 11th Integrative Health Conference on Friday evening.

But the main event was Saturday evening - a gala dinner and concert of Newton-John's music from her album "Grace and Gratitude." It would be the first time that she would perform the entire album in concert.

"I've never performed it as a concert before," said Newton-John. "It's all original material [that she co-wrote with Amy Sky]. I've done maybe two or three songs off the album in my shows, but I have never done it as a whole concert. So it's a whole different way for me to go. The songs are really important to me because they connected me to my husband."

That would be John Easterling, her second husband, founder and president of the Amazon Herb Company, a natural remedy firm. The two had been friends for years before they married.

"He came to a show of mine that I had invited him to and heard these songs and felt they were so human that he wanted to take me to the Amazon," said

Newton-John. "He invited me to go down there and that's what kind of connected us. So it's kind of full circle."

Newton-John and Easterling have been supporters of ACEER for years. The president of the nonprofit organization, which has worked for rainforest conservation and community education in the Peruvian Amazon, is Roger Mustalish, who has an office at West Chester University. It was through Newton-John and Easterling's connection with Mustalish that the health, wellness and environmental conservation event came about.

"It's a big shock to any woman — or man — when they find out they have breast cancer," said Newton-John. "I found that I mixed the Western therapies and the Eastern therapies and that really helped me greatly. I went through chemotherapy and surgery, but I also used herbs, acupuncture, meditation and visualization, all the things that would help my spirit as well."

With a career that has spanned four decades, Newton-John has sold more than 50 million albums, is a four-time Grammy Award winner who has had five No. 1 hits, including "Physical" in 1981.

"Not everyone is as healthy as I am and I am very fortunate," said Newton-John. "Cancer is not necessarily a death sentence and you can survive it. I just feel incredibly grateful and positive about it that I can help others and create this wonderful cancer and wellness center. The wellness kind of balances the word 'cancer' that scares so many people."

Fortunately for me, there was some new news on the Olivia Newton-John front right before our interview. She had just completed filming a cameo for an upcoming appearance on the Fox television show "Glee" when word surfaced that her 1981 No. 1 hit "Physical" had been named the "sexiest song" ever by the music publication Billboard.

Dancing in My Underwear

"I thought it was a hoot. I got emails from all over the world," said Newton-John. "I just did an episode of 'Glee' and we did 'Physical' on that show. No one really knew this was going to happen at the same time but it happened in the same week."

At that time in the early 1980s, "Physical" was a bit more risqué than what Newton-John had been known for at that point in her career. The video that accompanied the single featured a leotard-clad Newton-John working out in a gym with several overweight men who eventually turn into more muscular, younger men.

The overt sexual connotations of the song's lyrics reportedly were the reason the video was shot as a sort of workout video, a fact confirmed by Newton-John nearly 30 years later.

"That's why we shot it that way, because the song was so sexy," said Newton-John. "I suddenly freaked out and said, 'We have to do something to go against [that sexuality]! We have to do a workout video!' That's how it happened and it made the song even bigger.

"I think it's really hysterical," Newton-John said of the song's designation. "I love it."

Not only that but Newton-John's popularity continues to transcend generations of fans who still watch and enjoy "Grease," the 1978 mega-hit in which she co-starred with John Travolta.

"I think if we knew that it was going to be such a big deal, we'd make more films like that," she said. "We had a wonderful time making it. It was a great film and we had a blast. The music is terrific, the dancing was fun.

"There is just something magic about it I guess. I'm delighted that people still love it."

The Blonde Accountant and I attended Newton-John's "Grace and Gratitude" concert at West Chester University that Saturday evening in March 2010. It was, of course, fabulous. Unfortunately we did not get to meet Olivia that evening, and I would have liked that very much.

And thanks to my childhood friend Rick Cook, I'm pretty sure that had I met Olivia Newton-John, I would have had no urge whatsoever to pelt her with an apple.

Cheech and Chong
Tommy Chong
The Eighth-Grade Stupid Shit Hall of Fame

Back before the advent of the Internet and cell phones, junior high boys had to be more creative when it came to entertaining themselves. And nobody was better at that than my pal, Gary Psinas.

Gary and I had first met while playing Little League in Pekin. He went to school in town; I attended elementary school in the rural area outside of Pekin at Rankin Grade School. From first grade through eighth grade – our school didn't offer kindergarten when I started school in the mid-1960s – I went to the same school in the same building. My dad just happened to be the superintendent of the school. Yep, I was the superintendent's kid.

And he was the boss in those days. Judge, jury and executioner. I still remember the instructions he gave the 6-year-old me on the first day of first grade: "Young man, if you get in trouble at school, you're going to get in trouble again when I get home."

I was no brain surgeon, but even at age 6, that didn't sound like a very good deal to me. I was put on notice that every time I misbehaved, I was getting two for the price of one in the punishment department. Thank you, sir, I do not want another.

By the time I got to eighth grade in 1973, I had a spotless record of good behavior. But I was getting the itch to grow up and spread my wings a little bit.

Gary played a big role in that. It wasn't that he corrupted me – I think we corrupted each other about equally – it's just that we shared the same sense of humor. And that sense of humor was purely thinking up the stupidest 14-

33

year-old shit that we could think up. If there was an Eighth Grade Stupi
Shit Hall of Fame, Gary and I would have been elected unanimously on th
first-ballot.

Gary matured faster than I did. In the eighth grade, he had the bushie:
sideburns of any kid in school. He had better sideburns than his dad. I hadn
yet started to shave.

And not only did Gary always have the coolest stuff, he seemed to alway
have it before anybody else - certainly before me. He was the first kid
knew who had a mini-bike, but it wasn't just any old mini-bike. He had
"Chopper" mini-bike. By the time I got done talking my dad into getting m
a mini-bike, the best I could negotiate was a plain blue-framed one fror
Kmart. It had no style whatsoever. Believe me, it was difficult in 1973 t
impress 14-year-old girls on a Kmart blue mini-bike when one is ridin
alongside a guy on a chopper mini-bike sporting Elvis sideburns, all th
while singing the "Say Whaaaa Song."

I would try to describe the "Say Whaaaa Song" to you, but it defies writte
description. It's an audio-visual experience only. But suffice to say that
squarely fell into the Stupid Shit That 14-Year-Old Boys Think U
category, and quite likely would be at the top of the list were you to actuall
hear it.

Gary also had the coolest bedroom of any 14-year-old. His parents, Al an
Hilda (Gary called her "Hild") had allowed him to decorate it himself whe
he was 12. He painted three of the walls red, white and blue, and painted a
American flag that covered the entire fourth wall. Dyed fish nets (not fishn
stockings but actual fish nets) hung from the ceiling and he had a poster c
Raquel Welch – the one where she's wearing the cavewoman skin from th
1966 movie "One Million Years B.C." - which he decided to hang on th
wall on the inside of his closet so that Hild wouldn't see it. As I recall, tha

fooled her for about a week, after which I think he had to take it down and burn it.

What Gary did have, though, that no other kid I knew at that age had was a stash of Playboy magazines that he kept in a padlocked locker right next to his bed. Hild would have had a stroke right on the spot if she knew what was inside that locker. It's no wonder I spent so much time at Gary's house.

Apparently he didn't mind coming over to my house either. That's because he somehow found a stash of Playboys in my dad's closet in my folks' bedroom. I used to set up camp in that closet. I don't know how I missed finding that treasure trove of treasured chests.

And it was on one of those overnight stays at my house that Gary decided to swipe one of my dad's girlie magazines to take home. But instead of putting it with the rest of the Playboys in the padlocked locker in his bedroom where Hild wouldn't find it, he left it under his bed, an area that snoopy moms are less likely to find padlocked.

Well, Hild was waiting for him with the evidence – my dad's Playboy magazine – when Gary got home from school one day. She gave him seven kinds of hell, told him that he had been raised better than that and he should be ashamed of himself. She then informed him that she was going to throw the magazine away, but had changed her mind and decided to wait until he got home from school so the both of them could burn the magazine. My dad's magazine. That I hadn't yet seen myself.

Gary decided it was time to fess up. He told Hild that it was fine with him if they burned the magazine, but that it would probably be better if he returned it to the person from whom it was "borrowed."

"Who's that?" she asked.

Dancing in My Underwear

"Mr. Morsch," said Gary.

For several moments, there was silence. Then Hild handed the magazine back to Gary, and in a barely audible voice said, "OK, just return it then." Gary really did have all the best stuff before me . . . even my dad's adult magazines.

Gary and I were always on the same page when it came to what the adults of that era would probably call tasteless humor. Enter Cheech Marin and Tommy Chong.

Cheech and Chong's comedy albums put us on the floor, despite the frequent drug references. In fact, neither Gary nor I were into drugs – we were goofballs – so even though we knew it was drug culture humor, we really didn't see it as drug culture humor. We just saw it as really stupid and funny shit. And we had become experts, even at a young age, of what qualified as really stupid and funny shit.

As usual, every time a new Cheech and Chong album would be released Gary had it first. But since he lived in town and I lived in the rural area outside of town and neither of us was old enough yet to drive, it sometimes wasn't easy to get together on the spur of the moment and listen to the new album together.

But we each had access to a telephone. In our house, the first-string phone was a wall model that hung in the kitchen – Kmart blue in color. Go figure. The blue mini-bike should have come as no surprise to me.

But my folks had another telephone in their bedroom, one of those black rotary-dial ones, and that was perfect for me to listen to the new Cheech and Chong album – both sides, in its entirety complete with adult language and drug references – over the phone in the privacy of my folks' bedroom.

36

See, when I had the chance to go into my parents' bedroom, I decided to listen to Gary play a stupid shit record over the phone rather than search my dad's closet for Playboy magazines. I can't help thinking that Hugh Hefner would have been disappointed in my choice of youthful pursuits.

That's right. Gary would call me, put the record on and hold the phone's receiver next to the record player, pausing every so often to put the receiver back up to his face and cackle into the phone or offer commentary every time Cheech and Chong made a poop or reefer reference. We'd laugh and laugh until we were in tears. It was as fun a way to listen to a record as it could be.

And nearly 35 years later, I got to talk to Tommy Chong.

"Hey man, can you call me back on the land line? My cell phone is dying," said Chong to me over the phone. It was the same voice I heard all those years ago as Gary played those Cheech and Chong records to me over the phone.

Chong was scheduled to appear at the Keswick Theatre in Glenside in the Philadelphia-area debut of the off-Broadway hit "The Marijuana-Logues," a three-man show that addressed the rites and rituals of getting stoned. The show was a parody of Eve Ensler's "The Vagina Monologues."

"They let me do my own Tommy Chong-style monologue," said Chong. "It's not too far from my character. I really just play myself."

The thing that made this interview even more interesting for me was that Chong was just coming off a nine-month prison stretch in Pennsylvania. He had been convicted for his role in financing and promoting "Chong Glass/Nice Dreams," a company started by his son, Paris. Chong agreed to plead guilty to one count of conspiracy to distribute drug paraphernalia in exchange for non-prosecution of his wife, Shelby, and his son.

Dancing in My Underwear

"Going to jail is something I will wear like a badge for the rest of my life," said Chong in a telephone interview from his home in Los Angeles. "It's not often you get thrown in jail for being a protective father. But that's the kind of government we've been dealing with for a while now."

Not that "The Marijuana-Logues" itself hadn't caused a bit of controversy at the time. In 2005, the show canceled its spring tour because audience members were frequently lighting up during the show, according to published reports.

Because he was on probation at the time, Chong was barred from being around people using or selling illegal substances. And because that could have been in violation of his probation terms, the tour was scrapped.

And just a few weeks prior to that, Chong had given the keynote speech at the NORML (National Organization for the Reform of Marijuana Laws) conference in San Francisco. After the speech, there was a screening of Josh Gilbert's "a/k/a Tommy Chong," a documentary about the entrapment and incarceration of Chong on the drug paraphernalia charges.

Again, people started lighting up during the showing of the film.

"There is a no-smoking rule in the hall where the film was being shown," said Chong. "The security guys came in and said, 'You're shut down.' Pretty funny."

The Keswick show was billed at the time as the edgiest theater piece to come to the Philadelphia area in 2006. Keswick officials even put a disclaimer in their press releases that stated: "This production does not glorify drug use. Rather, it illustrates that cannabis culture is a thing of substance, humor and creativity."

Regular viewers of "That '70s Show" during its run recognized Chong in the recurring part of Leo, the stoned-out, aging hippie. Chong appeared in the second, third, fourth, seventh and eighth seasons of the show, missing some time due to his jail experience.

"I loved doing TV," he said. "I was supposed to be a guest star. Then I was a guest star every week, but they were still paying me like an occasional guest star.

"So I dropped out of the show for a year and then went to jail for a year," he continued. "When I went back to the show I appreciated it more. I treated it like a sitcom school. I watched the director and learned a lot."

Chong said he also had fond memories of the Philadelphia area, especially early in his career when he was a guitarist and songwriter in Motown.

"In the late 1960s, I played in South Philly as a member of Bobby Taylor and the Vancouvers," said Chong. "And Cheech and I used to work in a little club in Bryn Mawr. Philadelphia is one of the best cities in the country," he said.

On the night of "The Marijuana-Logues," at the Keswick, I had the opportunity to meet Chong backstage before the performance. In the brief conversation, I shared the story of how my friend Gary had played those Cheech and Chong albums to me over the phone as a kid.

"Pretty funny, man," said Chong.

He signed a copy of my preview story to me: "Mike, you spelled my name right . . . wow!" Alongside his signature he drew a smoking joint.

The whole experience of interviewing Tommy Chong and then meeting him before the show to tell him my story that connected his work with my life was something I could have never imagined as an eighth-grader.

The Doobie Brothers
Tom Johnston
Rush the stage and risk breaking a hip?

Our high school in Pekin, Illinois, was divided into two campuses – the older high school was called the West Campus and was for freshmen and sophomores, while the newer school, built on the other side of town in the 1960s, was called the East Campus and housed the juniors and seniors.

It was that way in the 1970s because we had nearly 4,000 kids attending high school in that era. Our class alone – the Class of 1977 – entered high school in 1974 with more than 1,000 students.

One of the unique characteristics of the West Campus was something called the Leeway - a long, wide hallway that connected the original high school building with the original gymnasium and a newer addition that was built in between to form one complete educational complex.

The Leeway was named after Jimmy "Doc" Lee, a longtime beloved athletic team manager who was unable to compete in sports himself because of his dwarfism. Doc Lee was a team manager when my father was in high school in the 1940s and was still there taping ankles and handing out towels when I attended school there in the 1970s.

But the Leeway was more than just a big hallway: It was the social epicenter of the school during schools hours. While its main function was to serve as the pathway from class to class for the students, its primary purpose during the lunch periods was to sequester all the students into the in-between section of the complex, away from those still in class in both the old building and the newer addition.

Dancing in My Underwear

One of the main ways to kill time in the Leeway was to pester the teachers who were policing the area – Mr. Marvin Kieswetter, a math teacher, and Mr. Michael Chobanian, an English teacher. And one of the ways teenagers pestered teachers at my school was to throw "hot" pennies in their vicinity.

The hope was that Mr. Kieswetter and Mr. Chobanian would bend over and pick up the "hot" pennies, which kids would heat up with their cigarette lighters before tossing.

That worked only once before the teachers figured it out. But it didn't dissuade students from throwing pennies. In fact, legend has it that by the time Mr. Kieswetter retired from teaching after years and years of Leeway duty, he had collected enough pennies from wiseguy students to buy a car.

My pals – Gary Psinas and Jim Oberle – and I had our lunch hour routine: we would head for the cafeteria to eat, spending the first 15 minutes of the lunch period trying to crack each other up with typical 15-year-old silliness. The goal for each of us, of course, was to do or say something funny enough to make milk come out of the other guy's nose. Oberle always lost that competition. He had so much milk come out his nose that year that I think the school was forced to hire extra cows just to keep up with the demand.

After the main meal, we would head downstairs and toward the Leeway, stopping at the snack stand – called the Dragon's Den – where I would usually grab a bag of popcorn and a frozen chocolate shake. Turns out the frozen chocolate shake was the forefather of what would become the Wendy's frozen milkshake, but we didn't know that at the time. All I knew was that it was going to be difficult for Psinas and Oberle to make popcorn and frozen ice cream come out of my nose, and that was part of the reason behind my junk food choices.

But the coolest thing about the Leeway was that the school administrator allowed us to have a jukebox. And nearly every day in 1975, I dropped quarter into that jukebox and punched in two songs: one was "My Maria," co-written and performed by B.W. Stevenson that peaked at No. 9 on the charts in 1973; the other was "China Grove" by the Doobie Brothers, which peaked at No. 15 on the charts in 1973 and was written by Tom Johnston, who also sang lead on the song for the band.

For a whole school year, a portion of my day consisted of lunch, milk out the nose, Dragon's Den, Leeway, Doobie Brothers.

And in October of 2011, I got to interview Tom Johnston and share that story with him - all except the milk-out-the-nose part.

"That's one of the things that lets you know that your music has stood the test of time," said Johnston. "It worked for people and they still associate it to a time in their life. And that's great."

But I wanted to know more about the song, and I asked Johnston to share some insight as the author and singer of that great tune.

"In 1972, we were touring in a Winnebago. We had started to hit but we really hadn't hit big. We were headed into San Antonio, Texas, at the time and we drove right past a sign – and I didn't see it, or if I did, I didn't remember it – that said 'China Grove,'" said Johnston. "My thinking was that subconsciously I saw the name 'China Grove' without having it really register in the frontal lobe.

"I couldn't tell you exactly the date I wrote it [it was on the 1973 album, "The Captain and Me"], but I wrote the words based on a piano lick by Billy Payne. And I made up all these ridiculous lyrics about sheriffs with samurai swords and all that kind of stuff. At the time, I still believed 'China Grove' was completely fictional.

Dancing in My Underwear

"So in 1975 I got into a cab, I think it was in Houston, Texas, and the cabdriver said, 'What made you write that song about that little old town China Grove?' I said, 'What town China Grove? I've never heard of a town called 'China Grove.'

"He said, 'Ya, it's right down there like it says in the song, right outside San Antonio.' That blew me out of the water. It really did," Johnston said. "That was a trip. I thought he was pulling my chain."

When I asked Johnston if he'd subsequently ever been to China Grove, Texas, given the popularity of the song over the years, he said he hadn't.

"I actually haven't ever driven through it myself, yet," he said. "It's a pretty small place. Like a feed store and an ice house or something to that effect, I've been told."

Since I had talked to Johnston to preview the Doobie Brothers November 2011 appearance at the Keswick Theater in Glenside, Pennsylvania, The Blonde Accountant and I had an opportunity to attend the show.

So when the band broke into "China Grove" during its encore, it took me back to the Leeway jukebox at the old West Campus of Pekin Community High School. It was all I could do to not rush the stage. I'm not sure why I didn't, except for maybe at this age, I figured I might trip and fall down the aisle and break a hip in the process.

In hindsight, I kind of wish I had rushed the stage during the performance of "China Grove." Even if I had fallen and broken my hip, it would have made for a pretty cool story about how it happened.

I guess I'll never stop talkin' about China Grove, whoa-oh-oh, whoa-oh China Grove.

America

Dewey Bunnell

Wardrobe malfunction:
Right guy, right spot, right time

In the summer after my sophomore year of high school, 1975, I hung out quite a bit with my pal, Dan Brewington. We spent a lot of time playing summer baseball for Coach Fred Reader, who when he was upset with us for making a boneheaded play, would call us "raaaazzzzberries," accentuating the "raaaazzzz" part. I don't know if Coach Reader meant it to be funny, but we got such a tremendous kick out of it when he said it that we would go out of our way sometimes in an effort to attain "raaaazzzzberry" status. A high honor indeed.

Hey, we were 15-year-old knuckleheads, so being described as "raaaazzzzberries" was probably the kindest thing that was said about us by various adults, including our parents.

But when we weren't playing baseball that summer, Dan and I hung out at the Sunset Hills swimming pool, with not a care in the world.

Dan lived in one of the higher-end neighborhoods at that time in my hometown of Pekin, Illinois. It was called Sunset Hills and it had its own country club, complete with 18-hole golf course, clubhouse and restaurant and a good-sized swimming pool. In that regard, it was not unlike Bushwood Country Club, the one made famous in the movie "Caddyshack," although that movie wouldn't come out for another five years.

One had to be a member of the country club to be able to utilize the swimming pool. Fortunately for me, Dan's parents were members, and the children of members could invite guests to go swimming. Guests were required to sign in and were allowed only two visits per summer. Well, Dan

had some pull with some of the various sergeants-at-arms who manned th
desk at the pool and oftentimes, I would get waved through even after I ha
exceeded my two-visit maximum.

The pool had a snack window, and Dan was big on the frozen Snickers bar
I think he ate a frozen Snickers every single time he went to the pool – a
least when I was with him - and I don't recall him ever waiting the standar
"no swimming for 30 minutes after eating" rule that was in effect during th
1970s.

Once inside the pool complex, various teenage shenanigans were always c
display. One such activity was called "Old Bag Splashing." We were no
exactly exercising the creative portion of our brains when it came to th
naming conventions of our activities.

"Old Bag Splashing" is exactly what it sounds like. In addition to attractin
its share of teenage boys, the Sunset Hills Country Club pool attracted th
fortysomething moms who would go to the hair salon in the morning to ge
all dolled up, then hit the pool after lunch for some sunbathing.

While lying on their stomachs facing away from the pool, which gave the
a perfect view of the beautiful second fairway of the golf course, a group c
knuckleheads, which usually included Dan and me, would slip into the dee
end of the pool, swim stealthily underwater to the shallow end where the ol
broads were sunning themselves, then pop up and start thrashing an
splashing about in the water, which of course soaked the women.

They did not like this much. But engaging in "Old Bag Splashing" was no
an unprovoked activity at all. It was in response to their incessant nagging a
those in our group on the golf course who had a habit "taking too large of
divot," whatever that means. I wasn't a golfer, so I didn't know these sam
women would lollygag around the golf course gossiping after each hole tha

46

they would complete instead of walking to the next hole like every other golfer on the course.

Criticizing teenage boys for their golf etiquette and then lollygagging about it afterwards is a good way to get wet, according to the guys in our crew.

Hey, it wasn't my golf course or my country club or my swimming pool. I was just a guest, albeit one who liked the idea of being a menace to polite society at every opportunity and had no trouble splashing about like a killer whale at a Sea World show when instructed.

But all that was just secondary noise. Being a guest at that pool one such sunny summer afternoon in 1975 turned out to lay the groundwork for what would become a milestone memory for a young teenage boy who didn't know much of anything about anything: It was the first time I ever got the chance to see a female breast.

Of course, in the mid-1970s, 15 was about the age that clueless young men from the rural Midwest like me started to think about something other than baseball and splashing old ladies . . . like 15-year-old girls. Really, what else was there to think about at that age? There certainly seemed to be plenty of girls hanging around the Sunset Hills swimming pool that summer.

And they were all wearing bikinis. It didn't take me long to figure out that was a good thing.

Even back then, though, I couldn't see past my nose and always needed my glasses. So when I was actually in the pool and trying to swim – I was much more proficient at sinking than I was at swimming – I would leave my glasses with my towel on one of the poolside chairs.

That, of course, meant that I couldn't get a real good look at the girls while I was actually in the pool. Well, that wasn't going to work for me. It quickly became apparent that looking at the girls was much more fun than actuall swimming, so a change in strategy was necessary.

I decided it would be better to see than to swim, so I would get out of th pool, put my glasses back on, and then sit on the edge of the pool, my leg hanging over the side and into the water. This provided me with th optimum site advantage.

It was a solid strategy for the 15-year-old me. I had been eyeing a youn lady in a red bikini, whom I didn't know. She didn't go to our high schoo so maybe she was the guest of another country club member.

I watched as she would swim the length of the pool and back, seemingl with ease. It didn't take long before I was mesmerized by her. Strikingl good-looking and an athletic swimmer, it seemed as if her every move wa in slow motion that afternoon.

And then it happened, all quite quickly. She finished a lap the length of th pool, then swam over to the opposite side of the pool to which I wa perched.

As she pulled herself out of the water and onto the edge of the pool in on fluid motion, her left breast slipped out of its holster and without he realizing it, appeared there in all its glory for what seemed like an eternity.

My first reaction was, "What is that?" followed a split-second later by " like that." Not surprisingly, I have had that same reaction to females breast for the past 35 years.

She was probably only exposed for three or four seconds, but it seemed lik an eternity to me. I just happened to be the right guy in the right spot at th right time. I was afforded the catbird seat for the entire show.

Once she realized that something was amiss, she embarrassingly made the proper adjustments to the bikini and all valuables were put back in their proper place.

I never approached her that day, never knew her name and never saw her again after the incident.

But I can tell you exactly what song was playing on the pool sound system at the very moment that I witnessed the wardrobe malfunction that turned into a coming-of-age story for me: It was "Sister Golden Hair" by the band America.

It was indeed the first time I realized – just like the song says – that "a woman sure can be a friend of mine."

And 36 years later, I got to talk to Dewey Bunnell, one of the founding members of America. He didn't write "Sister Golden Hair" nor is he singing lead on the song that eventually went to No. 1 on the charts in 1975. Gerry Buckley, another founding member of the group, wrote and sings lead on the song. But Bunnell's voice is on that record, and every time I hear that song, it takes me back to that happy and simple childhood memory.

At the end of our interview, I was able to share my personal story with him. "I would remember that song, too, if that was my visual at the time," said Bunnell. "I think that is a great testament for songs in general when they can take you back to a happier time.

"We always think that's what our job is during that 90-minute show every night – that we give people 90 minutes to put their heads somewhere else because those other problems are still waiting for you once you get home."

Dancing in My Underwear

It's been chronicled that "Sister Golden Hair" was titled as such because the mothers of all the founding members of America – Bunnell, Gerry Buckley and Dan Peek – were all blondes.

The only thing that would make my story better is if the young lady at the swimming pool was a blonde. Alas, she was not. She was a brunette. I think.

I really wasn't looking at her hair.

Three Dog Night
Chuck Negron
Elvis sideburns and a puka shell necklace

It was the spring of 1976 and I had not yet turned 17 years old. As president of the junior class at Pekin Community High School in central Illinois, one of my "duties" — in addition to running around being a teenage goof-off — was to help plan the junior-senior prom.

For the record, I was much better at goofing off than I was at planning a prom. But even having to suffer through bad clothes and bad haircuts throughout the 1970s, I thought I knew good music when I heard it. And although Three Dog Night had split up by 1976, I was a big fan of the band's music, despite having never had the chance to see it perform in concert.

So my big contribution to the prom committee that year was pushing for "An Old Fashioned Love Song" — written by Paul Williams — to be the theme of the dance. As class president with hip Elvis sideburns and a puka shell necklace, I apparently exhibited enough charm with the female members of the prom committee to get my wish on the theme.

We even convinced one of the parents who owned an old model convertible car at the time to park it out front of the school on the night of the dance so couples could get their pictures taken in front of an old-fashioned automobile.

I was also fortunate to have been elected to the prom court that year — a goof-off with Elvis sideburns who wore a puka shell necklace apparently also held some sway with the voting block of students — and I remember sharing a kiss with Sue Brown as we awaited our introduction to the prom

51

court pomp and circumstance. Sue didn't happen to be my date for the evening — oops! — but I sure do remember that kiss to this day.

And then 35 years later, I got to interview Chuck Negron, who sang lead on "An Old-Fashioned Love Song."

Three Dog Night — formed in 1968 and featuring three lead vocalists including Negron, Cory Wells and Danny Hutton — recorded and performed together until 1975. The now-famous name of the band was inspired by a story about Australian aborigines who, on cold nights in the outback, sleep with their dogs for warmth. The coldest evenings are known as "three dog nights."

According to Negron, Three Dog Night had some serious advantages on the way to success during its heyday.

"Not only could we sing better than anybody, but we had the best songs," said Negron. "And that translated into an unbelievable live show that was very successful. We actually did the songs better live."

Negron added that the band also had the good fortune to work with many great songwriters from that era — Elton John and Bernie Taupin ("Lady Samantha" and "Your Song"); Randy Newman ("Mama Told Me Not to Come"); Hoyt Axton ("Joy to the World" and "Never Been to Spain"); Laura Nyro ("Eli's Coming"); Harry Nilsson ("One"); Leo Sayer ("The Show Must Go On"); and Paul Williams ("An Old Fashioned Love Song" and "Out in the Country").

"They were great, great songs," said Negron. "When I heard 'An Old Fashioned Love Song,' the publishers weren't really that hot on it because they had Paul Williams writing with different people and he was very successful. This was the first time he had written by himself. So I said, 'Play it for me. I want to hear it.' I heard it and said, 'Hey, this is a good song.'"

So it was all those memories that were floating around in my head as Chuck Negron took the stage at Parx Casino in Bensalem, Pa., in October 2011.

Of course, there have been some changes over the years. Both Chuck and his fans are older now. I'd like to say that when the crowd got its first glance at Chuck during his entrance, we rushed the stage en masse. The reality is, our age group doesn't move that quickly anymore, so we collectively kind of shuffled up toward the stage. These days, we don't get close to the stage to rock out; we get close so that we can see and hear better what's going on up there.

Chuck performed all the Three Dog Night hits — "One," "Eli's Coming," "Mama Told Me (Not To Come)," "Out in the Country," "Never Been to Spain," "Pieces of April," "The Show Must Go On," "Shambala," "Joy to the World," and of course, "An Old Fashioned Love Song."

If Sue Brown would have been there, I would have kissed her again.

And for about two hours, we were young once again. Chuck can still rock the house and the graying crowd didn't miss a beat. With apologies to country crooner Toby Keith, we're not as good as we once were, but we're as good once as we've ever been.

Since I had interviewed Chuck for a story to preview the show, I was fortunate enough to meet him afterwards at the meet-and-greet.

I couldn't help wondering while I was waiting my turn to meet Chuck, watching him interact with fans whose lives he had impacted with his music, that there I was, about to shake hands with the guy who sang lead on a tune that served as the soundtrack for such a fabulous high school memory.

You'll swear you've heard it before

Dancing in My Underwear

As it slowly rambles on and on.
No need in bringing 'em back
Cause they've never really gone.
Just an old fashioned love song
Coming down in three-part harmony.
Just an old fashioned love song
One I'm sure they wrote for you and me.

You know, my back hurts, I'm going bald and I can't make it through th
night without having to get up and use the bathroom. But for a few hour
one night in 2011, my memories took me back to 1976 and there I wa
wearing a baby blue tuxedo with a fluffy ruffled shirt — the epitome of '7(
chic — with Sue Brown on my arm.

It may have taken 35 years, but listening to Chuck sing "An Old Fashione
Love Song" in person for the first time confirmed what I had alway
suspected: There's no need in bringing Chuck Negron back because he'
never really been gone. And "An Old-Fashioned Love Song" is indeed on
they wrote for you and me.

The Beach Boys
Mike Love
Washing one's hair in a toilet with Comet in the middle of Nowhere, Minnesota

My running buddies at Pekin Community High School included Jim "Beam" Beamish, Bob Walker, Dale Dover, Orville Gore, Jeff "Norm" Norman and my best friend, Greg Batton.

It was a witty group of guys who were above-average students. Mostly, though, it was a decent group of guys who really didn't get into trouble, despite our fondness for beer now and again.

Over a two-year period in 1976 and 1977, we did just about everything together: we played nickel-dime-quarter poker, rotating from one guy's house to another; we regularly attended professional rasslin' matches at Richwoods High School in Peoria; we had both intramural bowling (where we won the championship) and basketball (where we finished second) teams at our high school; and every once in a while we would take road trips together — trips where once we arrived at our destination, Beam was able to practice and perfect his projectile puking method of drinking beer.

Sure we liked our beer — like a lot of guys that age do — but we weren't into drugs and we didn't drink and then drive, but had rotating designated drivers. Sometimes, however, we'd drive a long way to drink.

Such was the case in the summer of 1977 after we graduated from high school. One of the guys in our crew, Orv Gore, had graduated a half-year ahead of us, at the senior year semester break. In general, this group of guys was academically more talented than I could ever hope to be, and Orv was near or at the top of that list, so much so because he was able to graduate from high school in only three-and-a-half years.

He did so because it was part of his parents' plan to retire and move from Pekin, Illinois, to Nevis, Minnesota. That's like moving from the sticks to the boonies. Just as a point of reference, the 2010 census revealed that

Dancing in My Underwear

Nevis, Minnesota, had a total population of 390 people, all of whom assume know how to fish. For all I know, it was the same 390 people wh lived there when we visited in 1977.

Our first reaction when Orv told us where he was moving was, "What th hell is a Nevis and is it anywhere near Frostbite Falls?"

So Orv graduated early and he and his family headed north. Orv wa planning on attending Bemidji State University to study moose and squirre. or something like that. He was gone from Pekin by Christmas of 1976, an we finished out the second semester and graduated in June 1977.

With nothing better to do, Beam, Norm, Bob, Dale, Greg and I decided tha for our senior trip — they weren't called "senior trips" back then — w would drive to Minnesota and visit Orv.

This shows how smart we were at that age. We did not for one momer consider that driving to Florida and looking at scantily clad girls on th beach would be more fun than driving to Minnesota and watching Orv's da sit in a boat and fish.

So we all hopped in Greg's dad's station wagon and headed north, awa from anything that resembled a beach full of girls. We loaded down th station wagon with our favorite beverage — at the time we were very muc into Olympia beer — and stocked up on the eight-track cassettes, one c which we absolutely wore out on the long drive: an album by the Beac boys called "Endless Summer."

A collection of Beach Boys' hits from earlier in the band's career – reportedly named "Endless Summer" by one of the group's co-founder: Mike Love — the album had been released in June 1974 and it put th Beach Boys back in the public eye for the first time since their successes i the early to mid-1960s. The record spent 155 weeks on the Billboard albur chart, made it to No. 1, and ended up selling more than three million copies

I always like the cover art on that album and didn't realize until years late that, although the album contained songs from the band's 1960s Beac

Boys' library, the cover art reflected images of the band members and how they looked in the 1970s.

We liked that album a lot. Lucky for us, too, because Middle of Nowhere, Illinois, was a long drive from Middle of Nowhere, Minnesota. And when we finally got to Nevis, there was a lot of sitting around doing nothing.

Fortunately, we had realized on the long drive that Dale was actually the best air seatbelt player (a variation of the air guitar) of the bunch, a skill that no doubt has improved his lot in life over the years. So at the very least, the trip had provided Dale with a new marketable skill.

Orv's parents, Tom and Etta, were quite pleasant people and Mr. Gore had worked hard his entire life for the opportunity to retire to the middle of nowhere.

The Gore home was located down a gravel lane overlooking a beautiful lake in a heavily wooded area. The neighbors were a good 50 to 60 yards away and barely visible through the trees. It would have been tough to navigate even sober.

The nearest tavern was about 20 miles away. We went there once during the weeklong stay and it wasn't worth a return trip. The most exciting thing that happened that evening was that Bob had given Jeff $20 that he owed him, but the thin Minnesota night air combined with the tavern's refreshments had convinced Jeff that the money was fake, so he tossed it out the window of the car on trip back to Orv's house.

That only left lounging around in the middle of nowhere watching Orv's dad sit in a boat and fish.

And drinking more beer.

One evening we were sitting around shooting the breeze — an Olympic-caliber spectator sport in that part of Minnesota — and before we knew it, the wee hours of the morning and the mass quantities of beer had enveloped us. It was as good a time as any to go looking for girls.

Dancing in My Underwear

At least that's what Norm thought. In yet another example of how we reall
didn't think things through at that age, the only girl within 20 miles of u
was the neighbor's 14-year-old daughter. We had seen her outside next doc
a few times from a distance and through all those trees, but the only thin
we knew about her was that she was a girl and that she was 14 -informatic
provided to us innocently enough by Mrs. Gore. Had Orv's mom thougl
about that for a moment longer, she might have considered keeping th
information from 17- and 18-year-old boys who had nothing better to do a
week than sit around her house and drink beer. In all fairness to Mrs. Gor
we were discreet with the drinking, as she likely would not have approve
of any shenanigans in her house.

So Norm decided that he was going to walk over to the young lady's hous
— at 2 a.m. and stinking drunk — and ask her out on a date. Although w
had a reputation of not exactly thinking things all the way through, the re
of us knew that was a bad plan.

But not Norm. He bolted through the back door of the walkout basement c
Orv's house and into the black night, intent on professing his love for a gi
whom he hadn't even met.

Navigating the dense forest that separated Orv's house from his neighbor
house in the middle of the night proved to be too much for the inebriate
Norm. Oh, he gave it the old college try, to the point that the rest of us wer
chasing him around in the dark and periodically tackling him to the groun
only to see him break free and try to continue the mission.

When we finally corralled him and got him back into the basement of Orv'
house, Norm decided that his backup plan of washing his hair with Come
cleanser in the downstairs toilet would suffice. That, we let him do. An
then we took pictures, like the good friends that we were.

At the end of the week, we piled back into the station wagon, convinced w
had consumed every drop of beer in Minnesota, and headed back to Illinoi
once again listening to the Beach Boys' "Endless Summer" the whole way.

And nearly 30 years later, in December 2005, I got to talk to Mike Love of the Beach Boys, the man who named that album "Endless Summer."

The Beach Boys — who by 2005 consisted of only original member Love and long-time keyboardist and vocalist Bruce Johnston, who joined the band n the mid-1960s when Brian Wilson decided to quit touring and concentrate on songwriting — had played the Keswick Theatre in Glenside, Pa., in April of 2005.

At that time, Love told the crowd that those who wanted to start a rock band ought to be careful.

"You may end up singing the same songs in the same key 40 years later," said Love.

This time the Beach Boys were returning to my part of Pennsylvania with "The Beach Boys Holiday Show," which included a selection of Christmas songs folded into a set that included all the Beach Boys' hits as well.

The Christmas songs included two — "Jingle Bell Rock" and "I'll Be Home For Christmas" - that the group had never recorded, as well as several classic selections — "Little Saint Nick" and "Santa's Beard" — from past Beach Boys holiday albums.

Love said that the Keswick Theatre was a perfect venue for the Beach Boys, as evidenced by the fact that the group had sold out two shows during the April visit.

"Theaters like this are designed for musical performances," he said. "It's good for us in particular because we're not a blues band; we're a rock/harmony band. In the Keswick, we can hear our own harmonies, hear what we're creating, unlike at an outdoor venue. Everybody can see us and everybody can hear us."

In 2005, the Beach Boys were performing between 150 and 170 dates a year and, according to Love, still getting great reactions from the fans.

Dancing in My Underwear

"If you look at the crowd — the positive, almost euphoric, response from the people — it's emotionally important to us as co-creators of the music," said Love.

That's because, Love said, the longevity of the Beach Boys defies logic.

"When we were starting out, there were a lot of one-hit wonders," he said. "But we felt early on that we needed to make each song on an album a good song.

"There was enough variety in our arrangements and it was entertaining enough to the ear that it didn't get boring.

"The thought we put into trying to make each song great I think led directly to our longevity," he said.

Listening to Mike Love — one of the guys who was there from the beginning of the Beach Boys — talk about why he thought the music had endured for so many years and through a couple of generations made me think about that trip to Minnesota some 30 years earlier and what a fun and carefree time it was.

The summer of 1977 truly was an "Endless Summer" of fond memories for that small group of good friends.

Hawaii Five-0
Al Harrington
Learning the proper way
to stretch a single into a double

Having never been away from home and on my own, going off to college in the fall of 1977 provided me the first opportunity to go completely out of control. Stark-raving batshit crazy.

My first college was Iowa State University in Ames, Iowa, a six-hour car ride away from parental control. It was there that I discovered the three things that all college guys quickly learn if they want to achieve a high-level of educational success: beer, women and beer.

I was also trying to make the baseball team as a not-scholarship walk-on. What that meant was that I showed up for practice every night as a member of what was unofficially called the "junior varsity" squad, whose only purpose as a unit was to serve as scrimmage dummies for the big-shot varsity team. We didn't have a real schedule with real games against other real junior varsity teams. We just got pummeled every night by varsity pitching, then retired to the local strip joints to drink beer and look at nekked women.

And yes, Iowa did indeed have strippers back in the late 1970s.

Our JV coach was a baseball lifer by the name of Leroy "Cap" Timm, the longest-tenured baseball coach at Iowa State University, who had led the Cyclones from 1937 until his retirement in 1974. By the time I arrived on campus three years later, he was already a legend and they had named the school's baseball field after him. But because he could never have walked away from the game after retirement, the school let him coach the scrubeenies hoping to make the big squad.

I learned a lot about baseball from Cap. I learned some good life lessons as well.

Dancing in My Underwear

Our ballfield, affectionately known as "the practice field," was beyond the rightfield fence of Cap Timm Field in a big open space. Right field of that diamond butted up against a set of dorms, separated only by a row of tall pine trees.

In the early fall, right after school had started, the girls from those dorms used right field as their primary sunbathing spot. So for the first several weeks of fall practice, while the weather was still pleasant, we'd get out to practice, only to find rightfield full of beautiful girls in bikinis sunning themselves.

The reality of scantily clad college women lounging about at our practice was not lost on young baseball players. I believe we all volunteered to learn how to play right field, and only a coach the caliber of Cap was able to explain effectively to his young upstarts that we could not field a competitive ballclub if all nine guys were playing right field at the same time.

So to eliminate any distractions from our ability to concentrate on baseball, Cap would lumber out to right field and approach the bevy of women, waving his arms and shooing them out of play and out of sight. He would then lumber back toward the infield and call us all together in foul territory, between home plate and first base.

"Gentlemen," he would say. "You cannot stretch a single into a double with an erection."

It was solid coaching from a local baseball legend.

By the time I got to my sophomore year at Iowa State, I had actually made the varsity team as a walk-on and was awarded one-quarter of a scholarship that I split with three other players. So in addition to beer, girls and beer, my educational experience now included being on a Division I baseball team. That did not leave much time for studying, as evidenced by my grade point average. Back in those days, we were on the quarter system, not the semester system, and our quarterly grades, based on a 4.0 scale, were sent home to our parents.

My father was an elementary school superintendent with a master's degree in education, and my mother was a schoolteacher. It's a pretty safe bet to assume that education was important to everybody in my family.

Well, almost everybody.

After the first quarter of my second year, I got a phone call from my dad in Illinois.

"Hey, how's it going out there?" he said.

"OK, I guess," I responded in typical teenager fashion.

"Have you seen your grades for this quarter?" he asked.

"No, how did I do?" I said.

"You got a 1.7. What the hell are you doing out there?" he said, his voice rising.

"Well, best I can tell, Pop, I'm playing baseball, drinking beer and chasing women," I said seriously.

"Young man, I don't think that's the reason you're there!" he said, this time raising his voice level just above a scream.

"I don't know Pop, I don't think it gets any better for me than that," I said.

I'm pretty sure that the unidentifiable sound I heard next was him trying to reach through the phone and smack me upside the head.

By the time I got to my second year in college, the movie "Animal House" was a huge hit and I spent a lot of time trying to out-Bluto John Belushi. In fact, I am the inventor of the "Co-ed Toga," which was nothing less than genius . . . that Wile E. Coyote-type of genius. Essentially, the toga was just a bed sheet. But the key was instead of wrapping the bed sheet around myself to make a toga, I found the prettiest girl I could find and wrapped both of us in the bed sheet. What this did was provide a cocoon in which to indiscriminately grope at will, totally undetected.

I had come into my own socially. And with one year of college and the "Co-ed Toga" under my belt, I became even more obnoxious, a quality that got me elected president of my dorm floor.

My roommate and I, Bill McBride from Meadville, Pa., had met for the first time on the first day that we had moved into the dorms a year earlier and we became great friends. We were sharing a room together for the second year as well, on the fourth floor of Friley Hall, which was called Meeker, named after a long-deceased engineering professor at the school, Warren H. Meeker.

It was a co-ed floor, which in the fall of 1978 meant that men and women shared the same living space. The women were at one end of the floor and the men were at the other. In the middle was the resident assistant's room — she was kind of the floor boss — and a room called "The Den."

"The Den" was for community use by everyone who lived on Meeker. It's where we held our weekly floor meetings, over which I presided, to address important floor business, like the weekly awards.

We had two weekly awards: The "Broken Pitcher Award," — an actual broken glass beer pitcher — which was given to the week's biggest and most obnoxious drunk; and the "Give A Shit Award" — a toilet seat — given to the week's biggest idiot who had done something incredibly stupid.

Needless to say, I was often in the running for both on a fairly regular basis.

But what "The Den" offered most for me was the opportunity every night after the 10 p.m. news to watch my favorite television show, "Hawaii Five 0," which by 1979 was still on regular network television as well as in nightly syndication. The instrumental theme song for the show, done by the Ventures, is to this day still one of the most recognizable in the history of television.

I didn't have a television in my room, and as president of the floor, I issued an edict - adhered to by absolutely nobody - that I was commandeering the television every weeknight for the show for one specific purpose: To see whether Five-0 chief Steve McGarrett (played by Jack Lord) was going to say "Book 'em, Danno!" to officer Danny Williams (played by James MacArthur).

I would cheer at the television if McGarrett said it, and boo at the television if he didn't. It became such an event every evening that around 11:25 p.m., just toward the end of the show, people from the floor, both men and women, would gravitate toward "The Den" either to cheer or boo along with me. The activity eventually attained a sort of cult status on the floor and became a nightly event.

As luck would have it, the spring baseball trip in February 1979 was to be 10 glorious days away from the Iowa snow in the sun and sand of Hawaii. The trip was scheduled to be taken during spring break, after the fall academic quarter ended and before the start of the spring quarter.

Just before we were to leave for Hawaii, my academic indifference caught up with me. To be considered a full-time student and thus eligible to compete in college athletics, one had to carry a minimum of 12 course hours per quarter. Well, concentrating on winning floor awards and watching "Hawaii Five-0" every night must have prevented me from actually learning the academic rules governing collegiate athletics. At mid-quarter, I had dropped some boring three-hour class and was only taking nine course hours. That meant that I was ineligible for that quarter, which didn't officially end until the start of the next quarter.

I couldn't play baseball in Hawaii. Unfortunately, it was a difficult lesson to learn. I only wish it had been the last boneheaded play of my life.

But, there was some hope. I was already booked, as were my parents, for the Hawaii trip. They were already paying their own way, and now I had to pay my own way. Fortunately, my dad showed mercy on me and agreed to foot the bill for my trip. As tough as he sounded, he had a soft heart for stupid ballplayers. He had been a college baseball player himself at Illinois State

65

Dancing in My Underwear

University in the 1950s, albeit a smarter one than he was raising, through no fault of his own. Of course, in exchange I had to agree to hit the books and never let something like that happen again, a promise I kept for the rest of my college career.

But I was going to Hawaii, and in an effort to turn a negative into a positive, I decided that I wanted to see a lot of the landmarks that I saw on television in "Hawaii Five-0."

I absolutely loved the theme song by the Ventures, especially during the opening credits, when the camera quickly panned in on Jack Lord standing on a balcony atop a tall building. That building turned out to be the famous Ilikai Hotel overlooking Waikiki Beach.

On one of the first days there, I traveled to the top of the Ilikai Hotel with the intention of standing on that very spot where Jack Lord stood, only to discover that I wasn't the only one who had ever wanted to do that. Because of the popularity of the show, the hotel wouldn't allow anyone out onto that specific balcony, so I had to settle for looking through a locked window a few feet from the exact spot.

But the highlight of the trip was yet to come. While looking at the local entertainment options, we happened across a dance revue show — featuring Tahitian fire dancing — at the Hilton Hawaiian Village in Waikiki. And it starred local entertainment legend Al Harrington, known to the folks in Hawaii as the "South Pacific Man."

It was the same Al Harrington who had starred as Detective Ben Kukua on "Hawaii Five-0" from 1972 to 1975.

There wasn't much doubt that my folks and I were going to that show especially after I begged them to take me. Why, my grandmother, a seamstress by trade, had made my dad and me matching blue flowered Hawaiian shirts and had made my mom a blue flowered dress that matched my dad and me. This show would be the perfect occasion to break out the matching wardrobe.

Even though he had left the television show by the time I got to Hawaii, Harrington had built up quite a following and another career as an entertainer on the islands.

It was a fabulous performance and I was enthralled at 19 years old to be in the same room as one of the stars of my favorite television show that featured one of the most recognizable TV theme songs of all time.

The evening was made even more special by the fact that we got to meet Harrington after the show for pictures and autographs. He signed my program, "Book 'em, Mike!"

And 33 years later, I found myself speaking to Al Harrington on the telephone, calling all the way from Hawaii.

"The fact that you came to my show [in 1979] and saw what we did . . . I'm not sure you realize this, but you helped me raise my kids," said Harrington.

"It was a show that told the story of Hawaii. We wanted to not only tell the tourist end of it but hopefully leave them with a little bit of history as to why Hawaii is as beautiful as it is," said Harrington, who taught high school and college history after graduating from Stanford University. "That was the whole general theme of the show. Not only to do the hula-hula thing. That's part of Hawaii's history but not its total history."

Harrington had played bit parts in the early years of the original "Hawaii Five-0," as villains, so when it came time to find a replacement for the departing Kono – played by the actor Zulu – as one of Steve McGarrett's cops, show creator Leonard Freeman chose Harrington.

"Freeman said, 'Well, we need another Polynesian guy and this Harrington guy looks pretty good. Let's bring him in.' I got the part without even auditioning. My bad-guy parts were my audition," said Harrington.

Harrington added that Freeman insisted on using local Hawaiian people in the show.

Dancing in My Underwear

"He had a tremendous feel for Hawaii. One of the things he did after th
show began to get its teeth in terms of the market, he got all the writers c
the show to come live in Hawaii. He told them that what he wanted them t
do was to write stories that had meaning for Hawaii and make Hawaii a
integral part of the stories. I think that was one of the great things about tha
show," he said.

Harrington added that veteran actor Jack Lord, who played "Five-0" bos
Steve McGarrett, took the part seriously.

"Middle America was buying his sturdiness as a crimestopper because ou
nation was through all kinds of problems with the Vietnam War," sai
Harrington. "The nation itself was looking for someone like that. I recogniz
that was one of the reasons the show hit. There was a sense of timing t
that."

Not that the show didn't have its lighter moments, despite Lord's seriou
demeanor.

"One day when we were filming – I can't remember what season it was
me and James MacArthur were bringing the crook in the door and Stev
McGarrett turns around with that iconic look on his face. He looks at me an
Jim holding the crook and says, 'Book 'em Dano!' Well, both Jim and I ha
rigged it so that we'd both look at him and say, 'Go book 'em yourself
Everybody in the cast, the guys running the cameras and lights, all buste
out laughing. It wasn't so funny for Jack," said Harrington.

"Hawaii Five-0" was revived on CBS in 2010, and Harrington has made
couple of guest appearances on the new show.

"I hope they give me a couple of others because I really enjoyed it," sai
Harrington, who is now retired. "I'm telling you this, though. What they d
for Hawaii cannot be bought, in terms of publicity."

As for the iconic "Hawaii Five-0" theme song, Harrington said it perfectl
captured the essence of all that is Hawaii.

"When I first heard it, my first impression of it – and I can remember rather vividly – I said to myself, 'Oh my God, it's artistic, it's got a feel of Hawaii. For me, I was touched by it. The song is one of those eternal things that's going to be part of Hawaii now for as long as Hawaii exists," said Harrington.

It was a real thrill for me to talk to Al Harrington about one of my favorite television shows and one of my favorite television theme songs of all time. That 1979 trip was the one and only time I ever got to Hawaii.

"You gotta come back," said Harrington. "Keep my card around, keep my name around and give me a buzz. I appreciate the fact that you remember coming to my show. You helped me raise my kids, I gotta take care of you."

It made me want to get on the next plane to Hawaii, once again shake hands with Al Harrington and thank him for being a big part of a wonderful memory.

KISS
Paul Stanley
Pinball wizard in a Mark Twain town

In early November 1979, my baseball career at Iowa State University came to abrupt halt: The coaches called me into the office and told me, "You're horseshit, we don't want you around anymore."

Baseball coaches certainly have a way with words.

But because I still thought I could play college baseball for somebody, I started looking around for a junior college in which I could enroll and be eligible for the spring baseball season in 1980.

That's how I ended up in Muscatine, Iowa, which sits right along the Mississippi River in the southeastern part of the state. There were a number of advantages in playing for Muscatine Community College: It was a few hours closer to where my folks lived in Illinois; all I had to do academically was graduate with an associate degree – a lot more difficult for me at that point in my life than it should have been – and I wouldn't lose a year of baseball eligibility if I then went back to a Division I school; and the home field outfield fences at Tom Bruner Field in Muscatine were considerably closer to home plate than they were at Cap Timm Stadium at Iowa State. For a guy who swung from the ass every single time up trying to hit the ball into the next county, short fences are what power hitters call "an advantage."

I found a place to live with three other ballplayers that I didn't know - Klaus Zumsande, Steve Prusha and Al Erger - in an apartment above a sporting goods store on Second Street in downtown Muscatine. We lived on the third floor, a group of four other ballplayers lived on the second floor, and our landlord Buzz was the owner of the street-level sporting goods store.

Dancing in My Underwear

We had several ways to occupy our time when we weren't playing baseball none of which included studying, all of which were stupid. When the mood struck us, one of the guys – usually Klaus – would climb up on the roof with a couple of buckets of water and dump them on unsuspecting pedestrians on the sidewalk below.

Or when the mood struck us, one of the guys – usually Klaus – would call the local fried chicken joint and order 25 two-piece dinners and have them delivered to an apartment on the third floor across the street, just to see the poor delivery guy schlep the 25 dinners up three flights of stairs only to have to schlep them back down three flights of stairs after he was informed that nobody from that apartment had ordered chicken.

Or when our baseball coach, Dave Huckleberry, would pull up in his suburban truck and park across the street from the sporting goods store and go inside to do some business with Buzz, one of the guys – usually Klaus – would call the local towing company and say he had a big suburban truck parked on Second Street that wouldn't start and could you send someone over to give it a tow?

Through all the tomfoolery, though, Muscatine was where I started to realize that maybe I wasn't going to have a career as a professional baseball player and that I'd better start paying attention in school.

I had done a sportswriting internship at Iowa State University while I was there with the city's newspaper, the Ames Tribune. When I arrived in Muscatine, I immediately approached the sports editor of the Muscatine Journal, Roger Bates, to see if I could write sports for him part-time. He agreed, and soon after I had my first byline on the sports pages of the Journal, the same daily newspaper once partly owned by Orion Clemens, brother of Samuel Clemens, better known, of course, as Mark Twain. The famous author actually worked at the Journal for a short time during the summer of 1855.

So 125 years later, I was following in some famous footsteps at the Muscatine Journal. I'm pretty sure, though, that Twain never dumped a bucket of water from the rooftop of a downtown building on the pedestrians walking below along Second Street in Muscatine, or if he did, he had the good sense never to write about it.

The other thing that used to occupy my time was pinball machines. I never was very good at it, but it sometimes helped waste away the some of the hours I should have been studying.

I had one pinball machine that I actually could beat every once in a while. It was just around the corner from our apartment in a little neighborhood tavern, the name of which I've long since forgotten. I never went there to drink, just to play the KISS pinball machine.

KISS – with original members Paul Stanley, Gene Simmons, Peter Criss and Ace Frehley - had been a pretty big deal for about seven years leading up to 1980, big enough to have its own pinball machine. But internal strife within the band was starting to take its toll. Record and concert ticket sales had started to lag and drummer Criss had performed with the group for the last time in December 1979, just after I arrived in Muscatine. (Criss did reunite later with the band again in 1996.)

The KISS pinball machines, which could accommodate up to four players and was manufactured by Bally, first came onto the scene in 1978 and apparently stayed in circulation well into the 1980s. The top of the machine featured cartoon drawings of the four members of KISS, with Simmons and Stanley front and center. The sides contained red flames dancing around the cartoon head drawings of the four. There were lots of bells and whistles, of course, just like all pinball machines. The playing surface of the machine was a mix of colors - mostly oranges and yellows – and KISS images and included the potential to score a 40,000-point "super bonus" and an 80,000-point "colossal bonus."

Dancing in My Underwear

One of those machines actually found its way to Muscatine, Iowa, and for whatever reason, it was one that I could handle and beat regularly. Consequently, I spent a lot of time in that little dive bar, usually around lunchtime, beating that KISS pinball machine like a dirty rug with little concern about the future, just simply enjoying the bells and whistles of a barroom pinball machine.

And more than 25 years later, I talked to KISS frontman Paul Stanley, but not about rock and roll or even pinball machines.

He called me from France and we talked about art. In fact, because of some other obligations, Stanley had missed an opportunity to go on a guided tour of the Louvre in Paris and ended up with time to talk with me.

I never had the slightest idea while I was looking into the image of Paul Stanley's painted face on that pinball machine that I would ever be having a conversation with him about art.

At the time, KISS was in the middle of its most successful tour of Europe ever in the band's long history, playing 29 concerts in seven weeks that was scheduled to conclude in late June.

The subject of our phone call, though, didn't have anything to do with music. Stanley was scheduled to make two special appearances at the Wentworth Gallery in King of Prussia Mall in July to display his artwork and meet fans and potential buyers.

"I look forward to painting," said Stanley in the telephone interview from Paris, a few weeks before KISS wrapped up the European tour. "It' something that I take a certain amount of . . . oh, I don't know . . . there is calming factor to know that at the end of this tour, I get to go into a room by myself and create from another part of my brain."

After reigning for more than 30 years as one of the most recognizable frontmen in the history of rock and roll, Stanley had embarked on a new career as a painter and had some considerable initial success, selling more than $2 million of his artwork in 2007. His King of Prussia appearance was part of an exhibition of his works touring the U.S. with the Wentworth Galleries.

"There are certainly going to be people who come [to the galleries] because of a connection that is first, and more primary for some, for what you're best known for. You're bound to have that," said Stanley. "I tend to say that my notoriety gets my foot in the door . . . then you're free to slam the door on my foot.

"But at the end of the day, having spoken to enough of the galleries and their owners, there is a good amount of people initially who are drawn to the work without knowing who did it."

Stanley said that painting has been a road to self-discovery for him and that he initially didn't paint with the idea of showing his work to anybody.

"The first piece that I hung in my house I found very surprising that people were drawn to it," he said. "They would ask me who did and where it was from. But I hung it because I was very pleased with it and the bonus was that it was moving other people.

"When it became obvious that there was a demand for my work, I absolutely had to make sure that the business aspect was taken care of. But business is only necessitated by success. I don't do things initially for the business of it. The business is something that is both a necessary evil and a terrific reward."

His art at that point was very much unscripted, Stanley said. He doesn't do preliminary sketches nor does he sketch on the canvas. He prefers to work

Dancing in My Underwear

"in a stream of consciousness and that way, the piece is as revealing for m as it might be for someone else."

"For me, the beauty of abstract art is that it's really ultimately about wha someone finds in it and that goes for me, too," he said. "I can certainly when asked at a gallery, explain my reality of the piece, but I will then te someone that ultimately what's more important is their reality of the piece.'

It wasn't the rocker's first venture outside the KISS perimeters. Stanley ha also achieved success and rave reviews on the stage, performing for si months in 1999 to standing-room-only crowds as The Phantom in th Toronto stage version of "Phantom of the Opera."

But after KISS had successfully toured Europe, it was all about the paintin for Stanley.

"To do a gallery show and be surrounded by works that I created that hav been met with such acceptance is very gratifying," said Stanley. "I'i blessed in that I have been able to take the intangible and make somethin tangible out of it, whether it's rock music or theater or fine arts."

He calls it a "road of discovery we all get to go on together."

"Painting is a very solitary and very intimate experience," he saic "Ultimately, it's shared, but the process isn't, so it's tremendously an deeply enjoyable because it's very profound for me.

"I've never done anything except to please myself, whether it's doin theater or doing KISS or doing painting at this point," said Stanley. "The are things I do very much for personal fulfillment and the icing on the cak is the accolades and pleasure that others get from it."

I did get a chance to meet Stanley during his appearance at the Wentworth Gallery in the King of Prussia Mall. Shaking hands with him, I couldn't help think that it sure was a long journey from that pinball machine in Muscatine, Iowa, to that moment.

The Beach Boys
Bruce Johnston
Face down in the fields of dreams

After putting up the best offensive numbers of my baseball career and also graduating with an associate degree from Muscatine Community College in the spring of 1980, I was offered a scholarship to play baseball at the University of Iowa, where I planned to continue more on the path to being a sportswriter and less on the path to being a knucklehead.

Although it wasn't in the scholarship deal — wink, wink — I also secured a job on the grounds crew of Nile Kinnick Stadium, home to the Iowa Hawkeyes football team. I hadn't yet found a place to live in Iowa City, but I was offered the opportunity to sublet a friend of a friend's apartment for the summer in Cedar Rapids, Iowa, about 25 miles north of Iowa City.

That was fine by me because, even though I was driving from Cedar Rapids to Iowa City every day for work, I was playing "town team" baseball in a very rural area full of small farming towns nestled within the cornfields just west of Cedar Rapids. In the summer of 1980, I wore the black and orange colors of Norway, population around 500, which along with other towns like Walford, Watkins, Fairfax and Amana formed the Iowa Valley League.

My dad had played town team baseball for his hometown of South Pekin, Illinois, in the 1960s, and I have wonderful memories of being a batboy for his team. That was back before the advent of aluminum bats, and as a little kid, I collected all the broken wooden bats from my dad and his teammates. The bats — a Willie Mays model, a Hank Aaron model, a Jackie Robinson model — were much too big for the little 7-year-old me to swing, but I nonetheless would haul them home for repair, hammering nails into them, wrapping the handles with duct tape and making them backyard-game ready. Never mind that the kids in the neighborhood weren't big enough to swing those bats.

Norway and its archrival Watkins had a big game every Fourth of July weekend, and even though the two towns didn't have 750 residents between them, around 1,500 people would attend that game. Fans would pack into the quaint little wooden grandstands behind home plate or in the wooden bleachers down each baseline. Those who couldn't find a seat would bring lawnchairs in which to sit or stand outside the chainlink fence to watch the game.

Really, there wasn't much else to do in that part of Iowa during the summer than to watch town team baseball. Every game was indeed a "Field of Dreams" kind of experience, several years before that movie was ever made. When I think about the times in life that I'd like to go back and relive again, I think of those three summers - 1980, 1981 and 1982 - where I played town team baseball in Iowa.

When I wasn't working at the football field during the day or playing baseball in the evenings and on weekends, life was relatively boring in Cedar Rapids in the summer of 1980. I didn't know anybody, and I was only going to be there for a few months until school started in the fall.

To kill time on those nights when I didn't have a game, I would just sit in the lonely apartment and watch TV, bored beyond all comprehension. In a misguided effort to spice up those evenings, I took up the use of smokeless tobacco. I was not particularly creative back then when it came to effective use of downtime.

Having not been a smoker — thanks to years of adolescent asthma and allergies that made it difficult to breathe in the first place — and not one to indulge in drug use, the smokeless tobacco seemed like a reasonable alternative to the 20-year-old knucklehead that was me. That was so because a non-tobacco user who suddenly decides to use tobacco can get as high as a kite with a pinch between the cheek and gum — for at least about a month until one's body adjusts to it. Well, that killed a third of the summer that I don't remember.

I never dipped smokeless tobacco while I was playing baseball because I could barely stand up when I was using it in the early stages. A lot of players in the summer league dipped. In fact, I once saw a guy in that league get hit right in the mouth with a fastball and the only thing that saved him from having to have his mouth rebuilt was that the ball hit him flush on the big wad of tobacco he had stuffed in the front of his bottom lip. All he got out of it was a split lip and a wad of chew down the back of his throat, a small price to pay, I think, for keeping one's teeth.

But baseball is a difficult enough game to play standing up, let alone trying to do it face down on the infield grass as the result of a tobacco high, so I never indulged during a game.

Fortunately for me, there was one other event that summer that kept me not only occupied but enthralled for at least one evening. And it was something that I would remember for the rest of my life: It was the first time I would ever have a chance to see the Beach Boys live in concert.

Having spent a good portion of my 20 years to that point listening to Beach Boys music, I was so excited at the prospect of seeing that concert that I didn't even need the smokeless tobacco to get high.

The show was scheduled for what was then called the Five Seasons Center in Cedar Rapids, a multi-purpose arena that could seat up to 10,000 for a concert. I sat stage left, up in the rafters, because I could only afford the cheap seats. Working for the football stadium crew kept me in gas, beer and potato chips, but not much more.

Dancing in My Underwear

Brian Wilson had stopped touring with the band in the mid-1960s, but a
the rest of the original Beach Boys were onstage that evening, includin
drummer Dennis Wilson, who sang a stunning solo version that night (
"You Are So Beautiful." Longtime smoking and drug abuse had taken i
toll on Dennis' voice by 1980, but that didn't make his gravelly solo an
less memorable to me.

I didn't know it at the time, but it would be the only Beach Boys concert th
I would ever see that included Dennis. He drowned three years later, i
1983, at Marina Del Rey in Los Angeles.

Nearly 25 years later, I was on the phone with Bruce Johnston, who was c
the stage with the Beach Boys that night in Cedar Rapids, Iowa, in 1980.

When Brian quit touring to spend more time in the studio, Glen Campbe
— who would go on to become a highly successful country singer in th
1970s — stepped in to fill the void left by Brian's departure.

But Campbell lasted less than a year with the band and was eventuall
replaced by Johnston, who has been with the Beach Boys ever since.

It was not the first time I had interviewed Johnston, though. In 1985 i
Rockford, Illinois, the Beach Boys had planned an indoor "Beach Party" f
media members prior to a concert at the Rockford Metro Center. Decked o
in a red and white Hawaiian shirt — which I might add was very stylish an
fashionable — I was part of a media throng that interviewed Johnsto
mostly because he was the only Beach Boy who showed up to the part
Everybody had to interview him because there were no other band membe
in attendance to talk to.

By the time I got him on the phone in April 2005, it was just me, one-o
one, with Bruce. He and Mike Love were the only two original Beach Boy

left in the band by that time, and the group was scheduled to perform a show at the Keswick Theatre in Glenside, Pa.

But just as he had stepped in for Glen Campbell, who had stepped in for Brian Wilson 25 years earlier, Johnston was pinch-hitting for Love, whom I was originally scheduled to interview for the preview story.

The longtime Beach Boys frontman, however, had come down with some bug and had asked Johnston to step in for the interview. At least that's what Johnston said.

"I think he picked up something in Mexico. He's shivering and sweating," said Johnston.

A Grammy-winning songwriter, Johnston penned "I Write the Songs" that Barry Manilow made into a big hit. During his career, Johnston has worked with other big names like Elton John and Pink Floyd as well.

At the time in 2005, Brian Wilson was in the midst of his "Smile" project. In 1966, Wilson began work on "Smile," which he has called "a teenage symphony to God." But Brian never finished the album back then for a variety of reasons, among them technical recording difficulties and a resistance to the project by other band members.

Nearly 30 years later, Brian decided to go back and complete the album, which was released in September 2004, and was touring in support of that album in 2005. In fact, Brian had performed a concert featuring music from the "Smile" album at a Keswick concert just six months before the Beach Boys were to take the same stage - the reason for which I was interviewing Johnston.

Dancing in My Underwear

"I mean no disrespect to Brian, but I think among his works, 'Smile' isn't his best," said Johnston in a telephone interview from in his home in Santa Barbara, California.

"Everybody is going nuclear for 'Smile' and I'm happy for Brian. But I see it another way. My ear tells me that his best work is 'Pet Sounds.'"

Johnston compared the "Smile" effort to the Miss America pageant, which was still being held in Atlantic City in 2005.

"Let's say you compete in the Miss America pageant in your 20s and you get down to the finals and then just stop," said Johnston. "Then you come back in your 60s and try to finish the pageant. 'Smile' is cool; I just think that 'Pet Sounds' is better."

As far as the 2005 version of the Beach Boys, Johnston said the concerts were still a lot of fun, fun, fun.

"It's the same key and the same vocal parts it's always been," he said. "The music always stays in the spirit that it was intended. It's fun to do the music and it's fun to do all the traveling."

And after all these years, the music continues to survive.

"There is no way there won't be an audience for this music,' said Johnston "Our legacy is a smile with harmony. The image is upbeat and happy. You can't ruin the legacy. I'm proud to be a part of it."

Roy Clark
Grinnin' with the ole picker and grinner

The spring of 1981 turned out to be the best season I'd ever had as a young baseball player. Having been unceremoniously given the heave-ho by Iowa State University baseball coaches in the fall of 1980, I landed at Muscatine Community College and played just one season – and it turned out to be my career year. So it turned out to be worth the ignominy.

I set five school offensive records, including home runs (21), runs batted in (67), at bats, hits and runs scored. It was good enough for me to earn a scholarship to play baseball at the University of Iowa in Iowa City. It was the right time to have a big year.

By the time I got to Iowa City, I was paying more attention in the classroom as well. And once it became clear that I wasn't going to get paid to play baseball for a living, I really started to concentrate on what was becoming my next first love: sports writing.

When I wasn't playing baseball, I was hanging around the sports department at the Iowa City Press-Citizen, the daily newspaper in town. My boss was a quiet and unassuming guy named John Cloyed, who had the greatest combination beard and mustache in the history of facial hair. But even more impressive to me was that John offered me a chance to write sports, covering high school games and writing feature stories about University of Iowa athletes who were not baseball players. John was encouraging and taught with a velvet touch, and I didn't realize just how much experience I was getting and how much I was learning from professional journalists outside the classroom until several years later.

I was getting $5 per story, and trying to write three stories a week. For a guy who didn't have two nickels to rub together in 1981, $15 a week was some

serious walking-around money. Why, I was even able to impress colleg
girls with that pocketful of money, all in $1 bills to make it look like I had
bigger bankroll.

For several years during the summers in the 1980s, the Amana Corporatio
– which manufactured household appliances like refrigerators and wa
founded in Amana, Iowa, about 40 minutes from Iowa City – would hold
celebrity golf tournament.

In conjunction with the tournament, the Oak Ridge Boys – one of th
biggest country groups at the time – would both sponsor and play in
celebrity softball tournament on the baseball field at the University of Iow;
the same field I was at every day of my college baseball career at Iowa.

In the early 1970s, the Oak Ridge Boys – Joe Bonsall, Richard Sterbar
Duane Allen and William Lee Golden – were a gospel group that ha
opened a series of shows for Roy Clark, who by then was well known fc
his starring role in the long-running hick comedy television show "He
Haw."

In 1977, the Oak Ridge Boys had switched from a gospel group to a countr
group and had started to hit big. By the time they got to Iowa City in 1981
they were a really big deal, having just released the album "Fancy Free,
featuring the No. 1 hit "Elvira," which remains the group's most widel
known hit to this day.

I had two writing assignments for the Amana VIP weekend in the summe
of 1981: For the golf tournament, I was to follow a foursome of famou
basketball coaches: Lute Olson, then the coach at Iowa; Johnny Orr, then th
coach at Iowa State; Don Nelson, then the coach of the Boston Celtics an
an Iowa grad; and the already famous Bob Knight, then the coach at Indian
University who was fresh off winning his second of three NCA;
championships just a few months earlier in 1981.

My second assignment was to cover the Oak Ridge Boys Celebrity Softball Game the following day at the Iowa baseball field I called home. Some of the celebrities scheduled to attend that game included baseball great Roger Maris and baseball Hall of Famers Stan Musial and Ernie Banks, so I was pretty thankful to have gotten that assignment.

The day of golf was relatively uneventful. In addition to covering the pro-am one-day tournament, then one of the stops on the Professional Golf Association tour, for the Iowa City Press-Citizen, I was also covering it for the regional Associated Press office in Des Moines, Iowa. Unfortunately, I could only get paid once, and my boss John at the Press-Citizen allowed me to work primarily for AP because its check for a day's work was $30 as compared to the $5 per story I was getting from the Press-Citizen.

Following around Bob Knight all day was about as boring as golf. Some in the press corps that day thought there might be fireworks with Knight in town carrying his second national championship in his back pocket. But Knight was friendly and pleasant and the Iowa fans – although not all that fond of Indiana basketball – seemed to like Knight.

The softball game the next day was more to my liking. I was a big fan of the Oak Ridge Boys at the time, and it was a kick to interview singer Joe Bonsall for my story. But I was even more excited to talk to Roger Maris, who then was only 20 years removed from breaking Babe Ruth's single-season home run record in 1961; and "Stan the Man" Musial, the most famous player to ever wear the "Birds on the Bat" uniform of the St. Louis Cardinals and a first-ballot inductee into the Major League Baseball Hall of Fame in 1969.

It was a dream come true for a budding sportswriter. And I wrote what I thought was the greatest sports story I had ever written up to that point of my career . . . about a meaningless celebrity softball game.

Dancing in My Underwear

One year later, in 1982, I didn't get any writing assignments for the Amana VIP golf tournament or the Oak Ridge Boys celebrity softball game. That's because I was actually chosen to play in the celebrity softball game, one of two representatives from the baseball team, along with assistant coach Steve Duncan. Each of the men's sports at Iowa that year got to name a few of their athletes to a team that would compete against the Oak Ridge Boys and their team of celebrities.

I don't think I got chosen because I was such a great player or a big name on the baseball team. I'm pretty sure I was the only one who raised my hand when head baseball coach Duane Banks asked if anyone wanted to represent the baseball team in the softball game.

So there I was on that day in 1982, dressed in the black and gold colors of the Iowa Hawkeyes – black coaching shorts, white knee socks with gold stripes at the tops, an Amana/Oak Ridge Boys celebrity softball game T-shirt and my Iowa baseball hat.

Pitching for the Oak Ridge Boys that day was Joe Bonsall, the very same member of the group that I had interviewed for my story a year earlier. In my only at-bat of the game, I ripped a clean single over the head of the shortstop and into left field.

When I reached first base, the guy playing the position for the celebrities was none other than longtime Oak Ridge Boys friend and country music star Roy Clark, whom I had been watching on "Hee Haw" for years.

In the true spirit of a celebrity softball game, he was standing at first base, ballglove on one hand . . . and a can of beer in the other. He was smiling that big smile that I had seen on TV so many times, especially during the "pickin' and grinnin'" bit he did on the show with Buck Owens.

Clark put the beer down and we shook hands.

Twenty-six years later, I was on the phone talking to Roy Clark, who was scheduled to do one show at the Sellersville Theater 1894 in Sellersville, Pennysylvania. At the end of our interview, I was able to share the story of when we shook hands during a celebrity softball game back in 1982 in Iowa City, Iowa. I asked him if he remembered those celebrity softball games.

"Do I remember? I sure do," said Clark, his voice rising in what I interpreted as his genuinely recalling the time. "I remember that like it was yesterday. Ernie Banks also played in that game. On the other team was the University of Iowa rassling team. You remember, the first baseman was built like a tank. Oh, Lordy, that is really something, Mike, that you would bring that up. Those are some very fond memories. Bless your heart."

Clark was scheduled to do two shows at the Sellersville Theater 1894 in September 2008. He was 75 years old at the time and still going strong.

And oh, yes, Clark, who is considered by many as one of the finest multi-instrumentalists ever to take to the stage in Western wear, was still . . . grinnin'.

"I can be walking down the street and I'll hear somebody from a block away yell, 'I'm a-pickin'! and I'm obligated to say, 'And I'm a-grinnin'," said Clark, who appeared on "Hee Haw" for 25 years.

"But I never get tired of pickin' and grinnin'," said Clark in a telephone interview from his tour bus on the way to a performance at the Muscadine Festival in Pelahatchie, Mississippi.

"When the light comes on and they introduce you, you know that's what you were meant to do."

Throughout the 1960s, Clark recorded several albums, toured constantly and appeared on television variety shows from "The Tonight Show" with Johnny

Dancing in My Underwear

Carson (on which he eventually became the first country music artist to guest-host the show) to "The Mike Douglas Show" and "The Flip Wilson Show." In 1969, his single, "Yesterday, When I Was Young," hit the Top 20 Pop chart and made it to No. 9 on the Billboard Country chart. Including that song, Clark has had 23 Top 40 country hits and in 1982, he won a Grammy in the Best Country Instrumental Performance category for "Alabama Jubilee."

And through it all, Clark's most endearing qualities - along with his easygoing attitude and rural sense of humor - have been his warmth and friendliness. The great Bob Hope once said to Clark, "Your face is like a fireplace."

"All those years on 'Hee-Haw,' I was in people's homes every week and I became part of their family," said Clark. "It's nothing for people to just walk up on the street and start talking to me. It's never 'Mr. Clark,' it's always 'Roy.' Some apologize and say, 'Oh, I shouldn't be so familiar with you but I just felt like I knew you.' Well, you just can't buy that kind of love from people."

And although he said that he couldn't imagine anybody walking up to someone like Frank Sinatra on the street and having a chat with him, Clark doesn't mind it one bit when people do it to him.

"You can't go up onstage and say, 'I love what I do but don't bother me when I'm offstage,'" he said.

Clark said that what people see onstage is the real Roy Clark.

"I have a good time onstage, I really do," he said. "The way that I act is the way that I am. I'm a little goofy, but that's good. Someone once said to me 'You're always grinning onstage when you're playing.' You'll notice sometimes I laugh at myself. I grin because I know I've made a mistake. When I start laughing, it means that I've made more than one mistake."

Raised in Washington, D.C., Clark is very familiar with the Philadelphia area. When he first started performing, he played county fairs and volunteer fire department fairs all over Pennsylvania and New Jersey.

And in 2008, from his home in Tulsa, Oklahoma, where he moved in 1947 with wife Barbara, his wife of 47 years, Clark was still touring extensively. His many good deeds over the years have led to his receiving the 1999 Minnie Pearl Humanitarian of the Year Award from TNN's Music City New Awards. In 2000 he was inducted into the Oklahoma Music Hall of Fame and he is actively involved with schoolchildren who attend the Roy Clark Elementary School in Tulsa.

Clark said the Sellersville audiences would be treated to a lot of special things during the shows, not the least of which is the seven-piece band that accompanies him.

"I have got without a doubt - and I've been privileged to work with some of the greatest musicians through the years - seven young people that entertain me," he said. "When we're going down the road and there's not a whole lot going on, sooner or later someone will take out an instrument and start picking a little bit, then someone else will join in. And they'll start singing and harmonizing and I'll just sit there and be amazed at how much talent surrounds me on the stage."

Once it dawned on him how much he liked listening to his supporting musicians, he decided to share them even more with the audiences.

"So I started featuring them as part of the show and it's one of the highlights of the show," said Clark. "I just sit back like a proud father and watch these kids. All of us up there, we feed off each other. We're so well-rounded that

Dancing in My Underwear

I'm confident in my heart that there will be something in our show that the audience will enjoy," he said.

I attended the evening show and was fortunate to get backstage to meet Roy Clark, for the second time. He signed a copy of the story and we shook hands. His grip was as firm in Sellersville, Pennsylvania, in 2008 as I remember it being in Iowa City, Iowa, in 1982.

And I went back to my seat in the theater, ready to hear Roy Clark do some pickin' . . . grinnin' after having relived that handshake experience so many years later.

The Boston Pops
Keith Lockhart
They sound just like the movie

In the mid-1980s, I discovered the Boston Pops orchestra. It was love at first sight.

I was managing editor of the Cardunal Free Press in Carpentersville, Illinois, a group of five small daily newspapers in the northwestern Chicago suburbs owned by the Shaw family, originally out of Newton, Iowa. The other papers were small dailies in Crystal Lake, Woodstock, McHenry and Cary Grove.

The Cardunal Free Press served the communities of Carpentersville (Car), East and West Dundee (dun) and Algonquin (al). Hence the name, "Cardunal."

The Shaw family had decided to combine all five of those small newspapers into one bigger, regional daily newspaper, which was to be named The Northwest Herald. Employees from all five dailies spent the better part of 1985 vying for positions at the new regional newspaper, as many people were going to lose their jobs when the consolidation was launched. All surviving positions would be located at the new newspaper building constructed in the centrally located community of Crystal Lake.

Fortunately for me, the Cardunal Free Press served as the guinea pig for what the new regional daily newspaper was going to look like visually. Thus, we had carte blanche to use any designs, colors and whatever else we could think of every day in the newspaper. The bosses would pick up the paper the next morning, tell us what they liked or didn't like, and through a process of elimination, my crew was responsible for developing the look of the new newspaper.

Dancing in My Underwear

It was as much freedom as I'd ever had as a young journalist in the first fe
years of my newspaper career, and as it turned out, the most freedom
would ever have the entire time I was in the business.

Part of the consolidation included a brand-new content-management syste
for the regional daily newspaper, a computer software system that offere
all the latest technology that newspapers could utilize for that era.

It was developed by a company called Atex out of Worceste
Massachusetts. Founded in 1973, Atex was a major software player i
newspapers at that time.

The company's training facility was in Worcester, and newspapers wh
signed on with the company had the option of sending their employees
suburban Boston for training.

In the summer of 1986, the long hours in the newsroom paid off: I wa
named regional managing editor of the new Northwest Herald and as such,
was one of four employees being sent to Worcester for 10 days to learn th
Atex system, after which I would come back to suburban Chicago and tea
the rest of the editorial staff what I learned.

Having never been to Boston, I was a little disappointed that I was going
be in the classroom for eight of those 10 days, leaving only the weekend
explore the area.

But I was a novice traveler and not much of an "operator" when it came
knowing and experiencing all the wonderful things that the big city
Boston had to offer.

Fortunately for me, the Shaw company had sent a couple of representative
to Boston a few days before I got there, kind of like the advance scoutir

team – a guy named Dennis and a woman named Kathy. And Dennis was an "operator."

The two of them picked me up at the airport on a Wednesday, and we immediately headed for the historic Faneuil Hall Marketplace. There we enjoyed the wonderful steaks at the famous Durgin-Park and its equally famous staff of playful and short-tempered waiters and waitresses.

The next night Dennis got us seats for a Boston Pops performance at Symphony Hall, built in 1900 and 99 years later, declared a U.S. National Historic Landmark. We sat in the second balcony for the performance, led by Pops' conductor John Williams.

Williams had replaced the longtime conductor of the Pops, Arthur Fiedler, who was named the Pops' first official conductor in 1930 and served in that capacity until his death in 1979.

The John Williams that I was watching conduct the Boston Pops that evening ended up composing some of the most recognizable film scores in the history of motion pictures, including the "Star Wars" and "Indiana Jones" films.

From the moment I saw that performance, I was hooked on the Boston Pops, and continued to follow the orchestra from my home in the heartland of the country for years, mostly through its Fourth of July and Christmas specials on PBS.

In 1995, Keith Lockhart took over for Williams as the conductor of the Boston Pops, where he remains until this day. And as big a fan as I am of the Pops, I'm a bigger fan of Lockhart. He is a wonderful conductor and a great showman, and I have seen him perform both on TV and in person, the first time at the Mann Center for the Performing Arts in Philadelphia in 2006.

Dancing in My Underwear

And then Lockhart brought the Boston Pops to my community, and I was o
the phone talking with him for a preview story about the performance.
The orchestra was scheduled to perform in December 2008 at North Pen
High School, one of the stops on a seven-city holiday tour of "America
Orchestra" as part of the Lansdale Community Concerts series, then in i
62nd season.

"One of the reasons I love touring is because people who have seen th
orchestra on TV for years, or who have our recordings, actually get to mak
contact with us," said Lockhart in a telephone interview from his home i
Boston. "Kind of the same reason a rock band goes on tour."

Boston Pops holiday concerts began in 1974 with three performances i
Symphony Hall in Boston. Since then, public demand for the performanc
had increased to the point that the Pops offered 32 holiday concerts i
Symphony Hall, in addition to its tour performances.

Taking the Pops on the road outside the New England area began in tl
mid-1990s, coinciding with Lockhart's appointment in 1995 as tl
conductor of the legendary institution.

"We have such a great product and it's such a part of Christmas traditio
for people in this part of the world that we thought a lot of other peop
[outside Boston] would enjoy it," said Lockhart. "It's been probably tl
most consistently successful tour we do."

North Penn High School was the only high school auditorium in which tl
Pops performed on that holiday tour.

"Columbia Artists does all the tour bookings, scouts the venues and dea
with the presenters," said Lockhart. "When we put a tour together, a lot of
is based on geographic needs. We have to route the tour in such a way th

we can get the equipment and orchestra to these places one night after another."

Although Lockhart admitted that playing big concerts in places like New York, Philadelphia and Chicago are fun, he said that he preferred smaller community performances like the one at North Penn High School for different reasons.

"Playing in the smaller towns is in a way more gratifying because it really becomes the focus of the community — it's the big holiday event in that community's season. And it's fun to be a part of what people consider to be their holiday tradition."

It's no coincidence that Lockhart always comes back to what he considers to be the fun part of his job. That's because he is indeed, having fun.

"It's genuine," he said. "It's also important to realize that you're doing this for your audience, many of whom have not heard it before. It's not just about whether I'm enjoying it; it's about translating my enthusiasm to the audience. It's only when I have a big cold that it's less pleasant."

Lockhart also was aware that economic times were difficult then for a lot of people, and he said that music can help navigate the rough spots.

"These are tough times for everybody," said Lockhart. "People's discretionary income is threatened, people's charitable giving is threatened. Our own endowments are down considerably.

"But there is more of a need for what music brings – a connection to our spiritual side, especially during the holidays. So far what we're finding is that people are very hungry for us, even in a very uncertain time."

Dancing in My Underwear

And after so many years at the helm of the Pops, Lockhart had become comfortable with the task.

"You're handed a 120-year-old institution and they say, 'Don't screw up,' and they're allowed to say that," said Lockhart in reference to first taking the job as Pops conductor. "It was a little bit intimidating taking something that had so much expectation associated with it.

"But the best advice I got was from my illustrious predecessor, John Williams, who said: 'Don't worry about running into this place and trying to change it and put your own impression on it. Make it part of you. If you're there long enough and are a good steward of the organization, eventually it will become part of you and you will become part of it.' That really has happened over the years."

The North Penn High School performance included a host of holiday favorites such as the Pops' signature "Sleigh Ride," the traditional "Santa Claus Is Coming to Town," and the world premiere of "The Polar Express," featuring the narrative and illustrations from Chris Van Allsburg's book and music from the film version by Alan Silvestri and Glen Ballard.

"I'm still excited and invigorated by doing this, so there is no reason to be anywhere else as long as I think I'm still contributing," said Lockhart.

The evening of the concert, I was accompanied by younger daughter Lexi who was 14 years old at the time. I wanted her to experience the same thrill of discovering the Boston Pops that I had years earlier.

And the Boston Pops and Lockhart brought their "A" game to the fans at North Penn High School that evening, delivering an early Christmas present to the locals with a big red bow of a performance.

Hey, this is the Boston Pops. Would anybody have expected any less?

I gathered from chit-chatting with several people at the show that Lansdale Community Concerts, Inc. had been trying for some time to get the Pops to come to town. Lockhart confirmed that onstage, later adding, "We hope that this is the first of several return trips."

What struck me most about the performance was the incredible amount of talent packed onto one stage in the auditorium at North Penn High School. That, and the fact that Lockhart — wearing his trademark holiday red shirt and red socks — and his colleagues were just delighted to be there and having a lot of fun, to boot.

To report that there wasn't a bad number all evening goes without saying. But I particularly liked the soft and soothing version of "It Came upon a Midnight Clear" and the innovative "Twelve Days of Christmas."

"Try as you might, you'll never hear a better version of 'The Twelve Days of Christmas'," said Lockhart.

He was right. That never was one of my favorite Christmas songs until I heard the Gloriae Dei Cantores' spirited version of that innovative arrangement. Where I come from, we'd say that the Gloriae Dei Cantores – who joined the Pops for this performance - can sing the stuffing out of a song. And we'd be right.

Another highlight was the orchestra performing the world premiere of "The Polar Express," to which Younger Daughter whispered, "Dad, they sound just like the movie." No higher praise can be elicited from a 14-year-old, I suspect.

Of course, Santa showed up, as he always does during a Pops holiday tour show, and the good-natured Lockhart played straight man to a handful of wonderfully stupendous, witty and funny jokes told by the Jolly Old Elf.

Dancing in My Underwear

Hey, did you think I'd ever take a chance of landing on the naughty list b
calling any of Santa's jokes lame that close to Christmas? I can't have tha
But ho-ho-holy smokes, Santa, who writes your material?

After the show, my daughter and I stood in the line waiting for Lockhart 1
come out and sign CDs. It was there that I was eavesdropping on anoth
conversation and overheard the Lansdale Community Concerts, In
president tell someone that, "This was the best concert we've ever had."

My apologies for eavesdropping, but I concurred with that opinion. Just 1
put an exclamation point on that sentiment, Lexi concurred as well.

Once we got our turn with Lockhart, he proved as engaging offstage as he
onstage, taking time to chat with everybody in line. While this may hav
caused a bit of consternation for those toward the back of the line because (
the lateness of the hour, it was apparent that Lockhart took his responsibili
of meeting with fans as seriously as he does conducting and promoting th
Pops.

I, for one, appreciated that and would have stood in line for as long as
took to meet somebody who respects the fans that much.

The Beach Boys
Brian Wilson
Little one who made my heart come all undone

I had just arrived at work the morning of January 4, 1988, for my job as state news editor of the LaSalle News-Tribune, a daily newspaper with a circulation of about 20,000 readers in north central Illinois.

The News-Tribune was an "afternoon" newspaper, which means it hit the streets around 3:00 each afternoon. By then, most daily newspapers had made the switch to being a "morning" paper, and the News-Tribune was one of the few left that had bucked that trend.

So we got to work early in the morning, between 6:00 and 7:00 a.m., and were done with the day's work around 3 p.m.

The call came in just around 7 a.m. and it was from my wife, Sherry, who was around 27 or 28 weeks pregnant with our first child.

"You'd better come home, something's wrong. I think we need to go to the hospital," she said.

St. Margaret's Hospital in Spring Valley, Illinois, was a small rural hospital with fewer than 200 beds. It was founded in 1903 by seven sisters from The Sisters of Mary Presentation, a group of nuns that had been booted out of France by an anti-religious government.

Our physician was Dr. Basilio Padilla, a South African of Latin American descent. A wonderful baby doctor with a gentle bedside manner, it seemed to me like he was always smiling. In fact, I couldn't recall ever seeing him not smile.

That is, until we got to the hospital that day. Dr. Padilla was not smiling. That was my first clue that something was very wrong.

After briefly examining Sherry, he said, "She's in labor."

"But it's way too early," I said. "What are we going to do?"

"We're going to try to stop the labor," he said, and with that, Sherry was admitted to the hospital and, within minutes, was hooked to an intravenous drug that was supposed to slow down and, hopefully, stop her labor.

By noontime, the early response was that the drug was working, so that allowed me enough time to break away from the hospital and run back to work to inform my bosses of what was happening. Since we didn't yet know the seriousness of the situation or how long we would be at the hospital, I was unsure when I would be back to work.

"Don't worry about it; take all the time you need," said the News-Tribune publisher, Peter Miller III. Pete was a second-generation newspaper publisher at the time. At age 25, a few years younger than I at the time, he was just learning the publishing business.

Editor Floyd Esche was equally considerate. In the 1980s, one got the feeling of "family" from folks at a family-owned newspaper. "Just keep us posted as to what's going on," said Floyd, a genuine look of concern streaming across his face.

I appreciated those considerations from the bosses, especially since I was in uncharted waters as a first-time dad-to-be.

It was extremely cold that day in the first week of January, and it was expected to get even colder as the day progressed. I grabbed some clothes and other items from home – we had yet to pack the bag for the inevitable trip to the hospital because we didn't think we'd need to for a few more months. In fact, we hadn't yet even taken the Lamaze classes, so I was really clueless about what was happening or my role in the whole thing.

Once back at the hospital, there wasn't much else to do but wait. Oddly enough, there were no other customers in the maternity ward at the small rural hospital, so we had the attention of the full staff.

Sherry was hooked up to the intravenous drugs for the rest of the day, and at about 5 p.m., Dr. Padilla came back in to check on the situation and he was smiling. It was always good news when he was smiling. He announced that he thought the drugs had done their job and that the labor had been stopped. He was about to head home for the evening, but would be in contact with the maternity floor staff throughout the evening.

I had alerted my parents earlier in the day that there was a problem concerning their first grandchild, but I called them back to say that the crisis had passed. They lived just more than an hour's drive south of Spring Valley in Pekin, a small central Illinois town with a population then of about 35,000. They had offered to drive up earlier in the day, but I told them to stay put until we knew what was going on.

Besides, the weather had continued to deteriorate throughout the day, and by early evening, the cold winter winds had picked up to around 50 mph and the wind chill temperature was in the neighborhood of 50 degrees below zero.

Fifty degrees below zero. Really, once the temperature gets to zero, what's another minus 50? It was so cold and windy that by around 8 p.m. that evening, I was going out every half hour and starting my car – and the cars of the two nurses working the maternity floor that evening – just to try to keep them operational.

103

Dancing in My Underwear

By 9:00 that evening, I was sitting in the hospital room absorbed in my favorite television show, "Wiseguy," a crime drama starring Ken Wahl.

Right in the middle of that show, everything hit the fan and life was about to change in a big way. Sherry had gone back into labor.

Dr. Padilla was back at the hospital by 10 p.m. and he wasn't smiling. He assessed the situation and called me aside. "We're going to go tonight. I've called St. Francis Medical Center in Peoria and a neo-natal delivery team is being transported by helicopter here right now."

The plan was to deliver the baby, then transport her back to Peoria on the helicopter with the delivery team, where premature babies could get better care at St. Francis Medical Center's neo-natal unit than they could in the underequipped rural hospital.

And they were going to make the trip in the middle of the night in minus-5 degree weather with winds gusting up to 50 mph. In a helicopter.

I called my parents to inform them, and their immediate reaction was to drive the hour north to be with us at the hospital. In a surprising moment of clarity for me, I told them to stay put. The weather was bad and the baby was headed their direction. Just meet the helicopter at St. Francis when it arrives.

By 1 a.m. on the morning of January 5, Sherry was in full labor. The medical team from St. Francis had arrived safely on the helicopter and everyone was headed for the delivery room.

Everyone except me. I was ushered into the "waiting room" for expectant fathers, which even by 1988 standards was already an outdated aspect of the process for new parents. Fathers had been active participants in the delivery room for years, but only as spectators yelling "Push!" and "Breathe!"

I was by myself in a waiting room in the middle of the night on a maternity ward that had no other business, with the future of my family in the hands of some skilled professionals. Fear and uncertainty overwhelmed me. It was the loneliest time of my life, and to this day, I don't like to be alone.

At 1:45 a.m. Kiley Brianna Morsch was born, weighing in at 2 pounds, 4 and one-half ounces and measuring 21 inches long. One of the local nurses whose car I had been starting periodically earlier in the evening finally came to the waiting room and escorted me down the dark and silent hall to the delivery room.

When I entered, one of the neo-natal team members was attending to the baby, while over her shoulder, I could see Sherry still on the table, being attended to by Dr. Padilla.

The neo-natal nurse had the baby's head cupped in her left hand, and with the other hand, was holding a small pink thing between two fingers that looked like the head of a ballpeen hammer. She was vigorously and rapidly pounding on the baby's chest with this instrument, which I found out later was made of foam rubber and was designed to loosen any materials that may have been clogging the baby's lungs. But Kiley was crying, so I took that as a good sign. She sounded like a newborn kitten crying out for its mother.

Just as quickly, I was whisked out of the delivery room and back to the hospital room, with Sherry quickly to follow. She had not been allowed to touch the baby after the delivery, and now we waited as the team prepared the precious cargo for the return helicopter ride to Peoria.

At about 3 a.m., the neo-natal team wheeled an incubator into the room. The baby was wrapped in what looked like bubblewrap and tinfoil, with only her little face showing. We were allowed to reach through the openings in the incubator to touch her before she was transported to the roof of the hospital and the waiting helicopter.

Dancing in My Underwear

"We'll call you when we get to Peoria," said the neo-natal nurse. Nobod
was guaranteeing that she would survive the trip.

I called my parents and asked them to meet the helicopter in Peoria and kee
watch over their granddaughter.

And then we waited for the phone to ring. While we were waiting, Sherr
described to me what had happened in the delivery room, how Dr. Padill
and the local nurses had actually handled the delivery and then passed th
baby to the neo-natal team to do the heavy lifting on keeping her alive.

The call came in around 4:30 Tuesday morning.

"We made it to Peoria and your daughter is being transported to the nec
natal unit," said the voice on the other end of the phone.

Sherry was unable to travel right away, but we decided that I would g
home and shower, then immediately head for Peoria. Before I left town,
stopped by the newsroom around 7 a.m. and told my colleagues what ha
happened and that I was headed to Peoria. I had split days off then
Wednesdays and Sundays – so that meant I could stay in Peoria two day
before I had to be back at work on Thursday.

Once again, publisher Peter Miller III told me to take all the time I needed
and I was off to Peoria.

My dad met me in the lobby of St. Francis Medical Center and w
embraced. For the first time in that 24-hour period, I was able to let m
emotions out, and I sobbed in his arms. I was unaware how traumatic it ha
been, how little I knew, and worried that it was my wife who was now alon
in the hospital an hour away from her baby.

The next two days were a blur. I was at the hospital for the entire time, only leaving at the end of the first evening to go to my folks' house to try to sleep.

The plan was for my dad and I to head back to Spring Valley late Wednesday night. Sherry was getting out of the hospital the first thing Thursday morning and riding back to Peoria with my dad, while I went back to work.

For the next five weeks, Sherry and I were apart. She stayed with my parents in Pekin, where she could be close to the hospital in Peoria and be with Kiley every day. I would stay in our apartment in Peru, Illinois – a little town located between my office in La Salle, Illinois, and the hospital in Spring Valley – and work. After my shift ended Tuesday afternoon, I would drive to Peoria and stay there until Wednesday night. I would then return home to work Thursdays, Fridays and Saturdays, leaving after the shift Saturday to drive back to Peoria, returning home again late Sunday evening.

On those days when I wasn't in Peoria, I would get regular daily updates on Kiley's condition. With premature babies, gaining even one ounce of weight is a big deal, and when I got news of that happening, there were always tears of joy.

It was on those incredibly lonely drives to Peoria that I turned to music to keep me company. And I found some comfort from an old group of friends – Brian Wilson and the Beach Boys.

I was drawn to the group's 1963 single "Surfer Girl," the first lines of which are "Little surfer, little one. Made my heart come all undone . . . ."

Kiley sure was little. And she had certainly made my heart come all undone. And on those twice-weekly trips to Peoria, when I could hardly wait to see her, hoping that she would still be alive when I arrived at the hospital, I

107

would pop the Beach Boys tape into the cassette player in my car and play "Surfer Girl."

Over and over and over and over. That one song. For the entire hour's drive from Peru to Peoria. And I would cry and cry until there were no more tears left by the time that I got to the hospital.

Six weeks later, we brought her home, right around her original due date, weighing in at a whopping 4 pounds, 10 ounces. And we were now three.

I had missed only two days of work that first traumatic week when Kiley was born, the week I was told to take as much time as I needed by the bosses. When I left the LaSalle News-Tribune in late December 1988, nearly a year after the birth of my first daughter, I was docked two days worth of pay on my final paycheck.

I have never forgotten that.

Eleven years later, in 2000, I had taken a job as the editor of the Times Herald in Norristown, Pa. I moved from Illinois to Pennsylvania in early July while Sherry and the girls – there was now a second daughter, Lexi who was born in 1994 – stayed behind to sell the house and coordinate the cross-country move.

Since I didn't know anybody in Pennsylvania, I spent a lot of time at work On those rare times when I wasn't working, I would usually explore the area or be at Veterans Stadium watching the Phillies.

That summer, Brian Wilson – who by then had been performing solo without the Beach Boys and with his own band for several years – was scheduled to play with Peter Nero and the Philly Pops orchestra at the Mann Center for the Performing Arts, an outdoor concert venue in Philadelphia.

I had seen the Beach Boys in concert more than a dozen times from 1980 through 1999, but I had never seen Brian Wilson – the writer and lead singer on "Surfer Girl," the song that had meant so much to me 12 years earlier – perform live.

I was not about to miss the Mann concert. I went by myself and sat in the back of the venue. It wasn't as important for me to see Brian close up as it was to hear him actually sing "Surfer Girl."

And when he did, it transported me back to those lonely car rides to Peoria, on the way to see my baby girl. I sat there at the Mann and cried and cried, just as I had so often 12 years earlier.

By 2004, I had moved on to become executive editor of Montgomery Newspapers in Fort Washington, PA. Brian Wilson was scheduled to perform that fall at the Keswick Theatre in Glenside, Pa. Not only was I going to get to see Brian perform again, but I was going to hear him sing "Surfer Girl." To make the evening more special, younger daughter Lexi was going to accompany me. At age 10, it was to be her first live rock concert. Kiley was a teenager then and was unavailable to go to the show that evening.

Brian's tour at the time coincided with his release of the album "Smile," a work he had started with the Beach Boys in 1966-1967 but had never completed. Up to that point, it had been called the greatest body of music that had never been released.

On the drive to Glenside that evening Lexi and I warmed up for the concert by listening to Beach Boys CDs as well as other solo efforts by Brian. Both my daughters grew up listening to Beach Boys music, so this was not at all unusual.

Dancing in My Underwear

The concert was all that it was supposed to be. We heard Brian sing "Surfer Girl," and now both my daughters had a connection to the song.

By the time intermission rolled around, Lexi was running out of steam. She asked if she could lay her head on my shoulder and "rest" during the intermission. It wasn't long before she had fallen asleep.

Once the concert resumed, Brian performed several songs from the "Smile" album. Lexi continued to saw logs on my shoulder, even as the concert crowd and the noise level got amped up.

Everyone stood for the last half hour of the show – except me, perfectly content to listen, look at the backsides of the people in front of me, and every so often reach over and gently kiss my baby's forehead.

When it was all over, I awakened her and we headed out of the theater.

"Dad, was that you I felt kissing my forehead?" she asked, mostly oblivious - as one would expect a 10-year-old to be - at the fact that she had just seen half of a Brian Wilson concert.

"Yep," I said.

"Geez, I finally get a chance to see a concert and I fall asleep. I can't believe I did that," she said.

"That's OK. You got to see the first half of the concert," I said. "You got to see Brian sing 'Surfer Girl.'"

"Thanks for taking me to the concert. I love you, Daddy," she said.

It occurred to me that with Brian Wilson onstage and my daughter's head on my shoulder, that was about as good as it gets for me.

What else could I do . . . but smile.

And then in 2008, I actually got to talk with Brian Wilson. He was planning his third stop at the Keswick Theatre in recent years to promote his newest album, "That Lucky Old Sun," which upon its release had debuted at No. 21 on Billboard's "hot albums" chart. It was at the time the highest Wilson had charted since the Beach Boys' "Pet Sounds" hit No. 10 on the Billboard charts in 1966.

Certainly I was nervous to talk with him, given the highly emotional impact his music has had on my life. By 2008, it was a well-known fact that Brian was not an easy interview. The legendary founder and driving force behind "America's band," the Beach Boys, had been a solo artist for many years, and his well-documented struggles with drug abuse, depression and mental illness have caused him a myriad of problems for more than 40 years.

When I picked up the phone and heard Brian's voice on the other end of the line, I was nearly speechless.

"Hi Mike, this is Brian." For the only time in my professional career as a journalist, I was nearly speechless.

Fortunately, I gathered myself quickly, and my more than 35 years of experience interviewing people took over.

It turns out that according to Brian Wilson, it's not easy being, well . . . Brian Wilson.

"These days, it's a little harder than it used to be," said Brian, not elaborating, in the telephone interview from his home in Los Angeles.

111

Dancing in My Underwear

But none of that took away from the fact that Wilson, then 66 years old, said he's happy and healthy now. And apparently, he liked the Keswick Theatre well enough to keep coming back there to perform.

"It's quite a nice play to play," said Wilson. "Philly is a friendly place and the audiences are very good and they participate."

The Keswick was one stop on an 11-city tour to promote "That Lucky Old Sun" that started Nov. 10 in Nashville, Tenn., and ended Nov. 25 at the Westbury Theatre in Westbury, N.Y.

"That Lucky Old Sun," described by various reviewers at the time as part travelogue and part autobiography — at times breezy and upbeat, but with moments of candor — revisited Wilson's early life in Southern California, some Beach Boys history and, occasionally, some darker areas that Wilson has visited in the past.

"I was playing 'That Lucky Old Sun' on the keyboards and I said to myself, 'I'm going to go buy Louie Armstrong's version and learn it,' " said Wilson who collaborated with multi-instrumentalist Scott Bennett on the composing and recording of the album. "I thought it would make a good spiritual central theme for the album. So that's what I did. The inspiration came from myself. I love the album."

The album also reunited Wilson with longtime collaborator Van Dyke Parks, who wrote interludes that Wilson speaks between some of the songs and with Capitol Records, which introduced the Beach Boys to the world back in the early 1960s.

"I'm real proud to be on Capitol Records again," he said. "They had the Beatles, you know."

Wilson has a habit of showing up at the Keswick about every two years. In 2004, his October tour stop here coincided with the release of his album "Smile," a work he started in 1967 but didn't finish until 37 years later.

In 2006, Wilson and his band performed again at the Keswick, this time promoting the 40th anniversary of the release of "Pet Sounds," considered to be innovative for its time and now recognized as the work that established Wilson as what many people call a musical genius. For that concert, longtime Beach Boys bandmate Al Jardine joined Wilson onstage for many "Pet Sounds" songs and at the time said that he could feel the energy coming back between him and Brian.

So local fans were familiar with Wilson's band, which included Bennett; Jeff Foskett, a vocalist and guitarist who has enjoyed a 25-year association with Wilson and the Beach Boys; Darian Sahanaja, an original member of the Wondermints and keyboardist with Wilson for more than 10 years; Probyn Gregory, a composer and multi-instrumentalist who has been with Wilson for 12 years; Nicky Walusko, guitarist and vocalist who has been with the band for 12 years; Taylor Mills, who has backed Wilson's vocals for several years; Paul Mertens, who plays saxophone, flute, clarinet and harmonica; drummer Nelson Bragg; percussionist, guitarist and vocalist Mike D'Amico; and drummer Todd Sucherman.

"They're great singers and they learn fast and they're good players," said Wilson of his band. "They play real smooth and good, man."

And are they better than the Beach Boys?

"Oh ya, much better," said Wilson.

Wilson said that the audiences are really into his music and he likes the way crowds "participate" at concerts.

Dancing in My Underwear

And he often is flattered and humbled when people approach him and tell him what his music has meant to them over the years.

"I feel touched by it and I say, 'Well thank you so much,' " said Wilson. "I'm very nice to people."

I didn't feel comfortable sharing my personal story with Brian. The interview itself lasted only seven or eight minutes, and I was disappointed in myself afterwards for not eliciting more information from him.

But it had been a long and emotional journey from that cold night at a hospital in Spring Valley, Illinois, in1988 to that interview with Brian 20 years later in an office in Fort Washington, Pa.

Just talking to him, hearing the same voice that sang "Surfer Girl" now talking to me through the telephone, completed that journey full circle.

It was enough for me.

Mike and his mom, Ann, are pictured here with Al Harrington in
Hawaii in 1979. These photos were taken after Harrington's dance
revue show at the Hilton Hawaiian Village in Waikiki.

That's Mike with the big curly hair interviewing Bruce Johnston, left, of the Beach Boys at a "beach party" for media members prior to a 1985 concert in Rockford, Illinois.

Mike meets Tommy Chong backstage at the Keswick Theatre in Glenside, PA, prior to Chong's 2006 appearance in "The Marijuana-Logues."

The Blonde Accountant, a big Barry Manilow fan, stands outside the concert venue at the Las Vegas Hilton with her birthday present in 2006 - tickets to see Manilow perform his Vegas act.

KISS front man Paul Stanley is also an artist. In 2007, he appeared at the Wentworth Gallery in King of Prussia, PA, as part of an exhibition of his work touring the U.S.

Barry Manilow performed in Philadelphia in 2007 at what was then known as the Wachovia Center. This was as close as Mike and The Blonde Accountant could get to the stage that evening.

Daryl Hall performed a solo gig at the Keswick Theatre in 2008 at part of his "Live From Daryl's House" tour.

Beach Boys founder Brian Wilson, left, and his longtime music director, Jeffrey Foskett, right, greet Mike backstage at the Keswick Theatre in 2009.

John Oates worked with Philadelphia singer-songwriter Carsie Blanton in October 2009 at songwriting seminar at the Lansdale Center for the Performing Arts.

John Oates has a special bond with the Sellersville Theater 1894, now a music theater. Back in his high school days Oates, a native of North Wales, PA, used to take dates to the venue when it showed movies. Here Oates poses with theater staff and invited guests prior to his October 2009 performance at the theater. At right is ST94 owner, William Quigley.

"Law & Order" and "Crossing Jordan" star Jill Hennessy and The Blonde Accountant meet before Hennessy's 2009 show at the World Cafe Live in Philadelphia. Jill Hennessy is also an accomplished musician and songwriter.

Mike hangs out with John Oates at the Sellersville Theater 1894. Oates, who grew up in nearby North Wales, PA, performed a solo concert at the theater in 2010.

Larry Ramos of The Association signs the album "Insight Out" for Mike after the group's appearance in 2011 as part of the "Happy Together Tour" at the Keswick Theatre in Glenside, PA.

Olivia Newton-John headlined a two-day event in March 2010 that focused on health, wellness and environmental conservation called "Olivia: Voices for Healing . . . Our Planet . . . Ourselves" at West Chester University in West Chester, PA.

Mike got to meet Micky Dolenz of the Monkees at the Parx Casino in Bensalem, PA, in September 2011. Photo courtesy of Parx Casino

Original Lovin' Spoonful member Joe Butler, left, and longtime band member Jerry Yester, right, goof around in the green room with Mike prior to the band's 2011 performance at the Sellersville Theater 1984 in Sellersville, PA. The two longtime musicians spent nearly an hour telling stories about their experiences on "The Ed Sullivan Show" and their dealings with legendary record producer Phil Spector.

Mike hangs out with Chuck Negron of Three Dog Night before Negron's 2011 performance at the Parx Casino in Bensalem, PA. Negron sang lead on the Three Dog Night hit "An Old-Fashioned Love Song," which was the theme of Mike's junior prom at Pekin Community High School in 1976.
Photo courtesy of Parx Casino

**The Blonde Accountant and Mike have become big fans - "Dan Fans" -
of Philadelphia singer-songwriter Dan May.**

The author with his daughters Kiley, left, and Lexi, right.

Daughter of Blonde Accountant, Kaitie Hughes.

Son of Blonde Accountant, Kevin Hughes, and Mike at Camden Yards in Baltimore in April 2012.

The Bellamy Brothers
Howard Bellamy
I could be perquaded

The house on Black Street in Springfield, Illinois, wasn't big, but it had enough room for two young parents and a toddler in 1990.

We had moved into that rental property just before my daughter Kiley turned a year old. It was a single-level ranch home with three small bedrooms, a living room and a kitchen. The unfinished – and, thankfully, dry basement – had plenty of space for storing the then-meager belongings of a young family. Although it didn't have a garage, there was a storage shed at the end of the driveway that had enough space in it to accommodate the lawn mower, a kiddie pool and a few tools that I never had any intention of using.

There was enough room in the unfenced backyard for a child to play, but not unattended because the yard backed up to a set of railroad tracks. The only thing that separated the yard from the tracks was a row of pine trees.

When the trains would roll by, several times a day, the whole house would shake. It was difficult to grab a nap in that house during the day because the frequency of the train schedule prevented any extended periods of sleep.

And naps were important back then. I was working nights at the local newspaper, The State Journal-Register, as a copy editor. I'd go to work around 4 p.m. and get home between 1 and 2 a.m. the next morning. But I was also taking care of Kiley during the day while her mother worked. And anyone who's had a toddler knows that the child sets her own schedule, not the other way around.

127

Dancing in My Underwear

So I'd get maybe three or four hours of sleep before Kiley decided it wa time to start her day. I learned quickly how important it was for children have a nap during the day, because it was an opportune time for old dad catch up on a few winks as well.

Despite that, it was a complete joy to stay home and take care of m daughter during the day. It was in that house, right in the hallway in front the bedrooms, where Kiley took her first steps.

She and I spent a lot of time in the spare bedroom, which we called th "baseball card room," because that's where I kept my collection of baseba cards and other stuff. We'd sit in there for hours sorting through ballcard I'd take some of the extra cards I had – doubles and triples of the sam player – and put them in a shoebox for her. She'd sit next to me as I wa looking through my box of cards and look through her box of cards, sortir and stacking them like she was a serious collector. Considering that I too her to a ballgame at Wrigley Field, home of the Chicago Cubs, when sk was only six months old, maybe she did have an innate sense of wh baseball-card collecting was all about.

Those days together also provided time to teach her certain things abo using words and listening to music. For example, we'd go through all th body parts and learn their names.

I'd say, "Where's your nose?" And Kiley would touch her nose with h finger.

"Where's your eyes?" And she's put both hands over her eyes.

"Where are your ears?" And she'd grab both ears.

"Where's your hair?" And she'd put both hands on top of her head.

128

"Where's your butt?" And she'd pat her backside with both hands.

But because dads can be goofs at times, there also was room for some tomfoolery when it came to educating the little one.

I decided that the anatomy lesson needed a big finish, something that would really impress Kiley's mother and the rest of her relatives, so the last question was, "Where are your brains?" For that, I taught her to extend her arms outward and shrug her shoulders.

Har-har, hardy-har-har. There's some dad humor right there. I don't care who you are that's funny.

The other thing Kiley and I did together during the day was watch music videos on television. MTV had been around for nearly a decade by 1990 and it was still playing videos.

When Kiley was just a few months old and still nursing, she would raise a lot of hell with me during the day while her mom was working because I didn't have the necessary equipment to satisfy a baby when a bottle just wouldn't do.

I tried everything to appease her, and the only thing that would work would be to sit her in her chair in front of the television so she could watch videos on MTV. But not just any videos, mind you. She'd quit crying only for Def Leppard's "Pour Some Sugar on Me," to the point where I had to actually videotape that song off the TV and play it back for her to get a break in the crying.

By the time she got to be a toddler, we were still watching MTV videos. One time, in another effort to impress her mother with how educationally productive we were being with our time during the day, I dressed Kiley up in her little bikini, wrapped one of those plastic Hawaiian leis around her

129

neck, stuck a pair of sunglasses on her face and then videotaped her doing hula dance while watching the Beach Boys' "Still Cruisin'" video.

It was just too cute.

In addition to MTV, we watched CMT – Country Music Television – whic essentially did that same thing as MTV then, which was to play videos. Ar one of our country favorite videos in 1990 was for the song "I Could E Persuaded" by the Bellamy Brothers.

That song was the first single released from the Bellamy Brothers' albu "Reality Check." It reached No. 7 on the Billboard country charts.

At the time the song was released, Kiley was still learning the finer points talking and pronunciation. When she heard "I Could Be Persuaded," she ha trouble pronouncing the word "persuaded." For her it came ou "perquaded," with a "q" replacing the "s" in the word.

For several years thereafter, if someone asked me if I wanted to c something, I would answer, "Oh, I could be perquaded."

So when the Bellamy Brothers scheduled a concert at the Sellersvil Theater in January 2009 and I was asked if I wanted to do an interview t preview that appearance, I didn't have to think twice: I could easily b perquaded.

When I reached Howard Bellamy on the telephone, he was at his ranch i Florida. And like most good old boys, he does indeed have a good old dog.

"But I doubt I live up to his expectations of who he thinks I am," sai Howard, who along with brother David — the Bellamy Brothers — had ju released their then-latest single in 2008, "Lord Help Me Be the Kind

Person My Dog Thinks I Am" off their 50th career album, "Jesus Is Coming."

Despite what Howard's dog thinks of him.

The Bellamy Brothers are one of country music's most successful duos, kicking off their career in 1976 with the No. 1 single "Let Your Love Flow."

"We learned how to sing in church," said Howard in the telephone interview. "So we wanted to do something kind of special, a gospel album, and it came very naturally to us."

And at that point, the "Jesus Is Coming" album had been well-received garnering the group its first two Dove Awards for country album and country song with the single "Drug Problem" (which isn't actually about what the title suggests.)

But it's the shelf life of "Let Your Love Flow" that has been consistent all these years for the Bellamy Brothers. The song again hit the charts in late 2008 in the United Kingdom — and had gotten to as high as No. 19 in early January 2009, ahead of songs by Beyonce and Britney Spears — thanks to a credit card advertisement for Barclay Bank.

"As much as that song has done for us, I never get tired of singing it," said Bellamy, who likened the Barclay Bank credit card to what the American Express card is here in the U.S. "It's just one of those songs that's a magical song. It has had an incredible life. It amazes us how it always pops up somewhere."

Although "Let Your Love Flow" — which was written by one of Neil Diamond's roadies, Larry E. Williams — was the group's first crossover hit, reaching No. 1 in the U.S., Great Britain, Scandinavia and Germany, the Bellamy Brothers' first No. 1 country hit was the Grammy award-winning song, "If I Said You Had a Beautiful Body [Would You Hold It Against Me]" in 1979.

It's always been like that for the Bellamy Brothers - that quirky song title kind of thing. Raised in Florida, and without any formal training, Howard and David mastered several instruments and started playing paid gigs while in college.

In 1973, David wrote "Spiders and Snakes," which became a top-five hit for Jim Stafford and went on to sell three million copies. That song eventually got them from Florida to Los Angeles and in 1975, a record deal with Curb/Warner Bros.

Following "Let Your Love Flow" and "If I Said You Had a Beautiful Body [Would You Hold It Against Me]" were other Bellamy-written classics like "You Just Ain't Whistlin' Dixie," "Kids of the Baby Boom," "For All the Wrong Reasons" and "Old Hippie."

"The writing is the best of all worlds," said Bellamy. "It's really a rewarding thing to have conceived a song and hear it heard back and become a hit all around the world. It's a pretty amazing process."

Bellamy said that he likes it when he knows the origin of a song and the story behind it, "Just to see where it can go from there." "Spiders and Snakes" is just such an example of that, and was written after a personal experience the brothers had at the Florida ranch.

"Many years ago, David and me went out carousing on the town when we were a little underage," he said. "We came in after doing things we shouldn't have been doing and didn't want our mom to know.

"We slept in an old bunkhouse here on our ranch. What we call a chicken snake got in my bed that night and when it found me, boy, I made a new door in that bunkhouse. Of course, being from Florida, there are always spiders everywhere too, and that song was written the next morning after that incident."

Bellamy also said that having a good sense of humor and being able to relax and enjoy music are important things to keep in perspective.

"It's a beneficial thing to have a sense of humor because you can only take things so seriously and then at some point, you just have to laugh about it," he said.

"We go to areas now and some audiences are getting kind of jaded because they've seen and heard so much," he said. "It's a good feeling to see people just have a great time and forget about what's going on around them. When you see that at the end of the show, that's when you know you've done your job."

Bellamy said that fans at the Sellersville show could expect to hear all the old hits as well as some of the new songs from the "Jesus Is Coming" album.

"We do as many of the old hits as we can because we still believe that's what people come to hear," he said. "And we throw a couple of new things in for our own entertainment that hopefully the crowd will like."

Over the years, the Bellamy Brothers have visited Philadelphia and its surrounding area a number of times and are acquainted with some of the local customs.

"Ya, we're familiar with your cheesesteaks," he said.

At the end of the interview, I was able to share the "perquaded" story with Howard, who listened patiently.

133

Dancing in My Underwear

"That's a funny story," he said.

The night of the Sellersville show, though, there was a problem. The tou
bus carrying the Bellamy Brothers broke down, and they were late getting t
Sellersville. While the patient crowd – seated and already having bee
entertained by the opening act - watched, the Bellamy Brothers' road cre
unloaded the equipment and instruments through the side door of the theat
and set everything up. About an hour after the scheduled start of the show
the Bellamy Brothers went onstage without a soundcheck.

And they sounded great, of course. It was the first time I had seen them in
live performance. And when they sang "I Could Be Persuaded," all thos
memories of young fatherhood came flooding back, along with a few tear
It was a wonderful moment of memories.

Given the chance to see the Bellamy Brothers in concert again, well . . .
could be perquaded.

The Beach Boys
Al Jardine
The right shirt at the wrong time

There's something about the Illinois State Fair. It's more than just sugared Tom Thumb donuts and corn on a stick, more than horses, cows, pigs, chickens, tractors, carnival rides and the Butter Cow.

Throughout the decade of the 1990s, the fair hosted some pretty good entertainment — most notably, for me, the Beach Boys.

My family lived on the north end of Springfield, which then had just more than 100,000 population and, aside from Peoria, was the biggest Illinois town between Chicago and St. Louis.

Those of us who lived in that part of town, not surprisingly, were called "Northenders." It was a typically middle-class neighborhood in a typically Midwestern town. It would not be a stretch to consider the annual state fair among the town's top social events of the year, even for the bib-overall-wearing crowd.

Every year, we tried to attend the fair two or three times during its 10-day run. My daughters were younger then, and they enjoyed the kiddie carnival and seeing the animals.

I, of course, enjoyed seeing the Beach Boys. At the time, I was working nights at the local newspaper — the State Journal-Register — so I had to get the evening off every time the band performed in the Grandstand, which took up a significant part of real estate on the north side of the massive fairgrounds.

Dancing in My Underwear

The Grandstand wasn't a great place to watch a concert. It was exactly wh its name implies - a big old grandstand alongside one side of a dirt race tra(that was built for watching horse races, not concerts.

The entertainment stage was constructed dead center facing the Grandstan across the dirt track and on the innermost portion of the track's infiel During concerts, the track area was used as a sort of mosh pit for those wl wanted to stand close to the stage for an entire show. When it rained, predictably became one big mudhole for concertgoers.

For those of us who always sat beneath the overhang of the Grandstand, tl weather wasn't usually a factor, but the sightlines were. It's no exaggerati(to say that some of those seats were 50 to 75 yards away from the stag much like a big football stadium concert.

To help people see the performers better, big video screens were erected (either side of the stage. When I say I saw the Beach Boys perform at tl Grandstand nearly a dozen times, what I mean is that I "heard" the Beac Boys perform at the Grandstand nearly a dozen times. I really didn't s(much of anything.

Beach Boys co-founder Brian Wilson had stopped performing regularly wi the band two decades earlier and never at the Illinois State Fair shows, ar his brother, drummer Dennis Wilson, had died in 1983.

But the rest of the original Beach Boys — frontman Mike Love, Ca Wilson, Al Jardine and Bruce Johnston — were always on the stag throughout the 1990s. And a couple of times, John Stamos — known for h role as "Uncle Jesse" on the long-running TV show "Full House" from 198 to 1995 — would show up and play drums with the Beach Boys. Stamo played the conga steel drums in the Beach Boys' 1988 video for "Kokomc and performed regularly with the group on its summer tours throughout tl 1990s.

It was a grand time in the Grandstand throughout the decade, listening to the Beach Boys . . . even though I couldn't see them.

And then a decade later, I got a better look — I interviewed original Beach Boys' guitarist and vocalist Al Jardine, who was joining his longtime friend Brian Wilson onstage for six shows during Wilson's 40th anniversary solo tour of the Beach Boys' legendary 1966 album, "Pet Sounds," with one of those stops being the Keswick Theatre in Glenside, Pa.

Wilson had kicked off the short tour Nov. 1 at UCLA's Royce Hall in Los Angeles. On Nov. 12, he was in London without Jardine. But the two reconnected again for the Nov. 17 show in Boston, the Nov. 18 show in Washington, D.C., the Nov. 19 show at the Keswick and then for two shows Nov. 21-22 in New York.

Wilson, with his backing band and with Jardine billed as a "special guest," played "Pet Sounds" in its entirety during each stop of the tour.

"This is a great opportunity to enjoy the music we worked so hard to create," said Jardine in a telephone interview from his home in California in advance of the Keswick show. "We really didn't enjoy it as much at the time because it was so labor-intensive. Forty years later we're getting some gratification, and that's special."

Jardine said that invitations to participate in this tour had been extended to other Beach Boys Mike Love and Bruce Johnston, but that "for some reason, it didn't work out."

"But that's not sour grapes," said Jardine. "So I just invited myself along with Brian. And I'm having a ball."

Longtime Beach Boys fans are familiar with the story of "Pet Sounds." In the mid-1960s, Brian Wilson decided to stop touring with the Beach Boys

and concentrate on writing songs. He had listened to the Beatles' "Rubb«
Soul" album and wanted to produce a better body of work.

In 1966, the Beach Boys — with Brian at home writing with collaborat«
Tony Asher — had toured Japan. Brian had "Pet Sounds" waiting for the»
when they returned.

"I felt competitive with the Beatles and I wanted to top them," Wilson sai
in "The Making of Pet Sounds," a video history of the album that is part «
the two-CD reissue by Capitol Records. "I knew there was a 'Pet Sounds' i
my soul somewhere."

"It was overwhelming then," said Jardine, of the type of music the Beac
Boys found in "Pet Sounds" when they returned from Japan. "It had a lot «
musical concepts that fused the old and the new. Really, in all honesty,
abandoned the formula that we were used to up to that point."
At the opening gig Nov. 1 at UCLA, Wilson and Jardine got some pret»
good reactions from the crowd.

"It was the first time that Brian and I had been on stage together for quite
while, the first time ever we had performed 'Pet Sounds' together onstage
said Jardine. "I had to fall into line and try to remember my parts. But it a
came back real fast. It's like riding a bike."

Jardine said that he was impressed with Wilson's performance. "He's singir
with feeling." And Jardine added that the California crowd enthusiastically
welcomed the California boys. Jardine's assessment of Wilson
performance was backed up by reviews of the concert and various Intern
message board comments from people who attended the show.

"It was a very humbling experience to be welcomed like that," he said of th
UCLA crowd. "I reciprocated by giving them a really good version of Phil
Spector's 'Then I Kissed Her.' I hadn't sung that one for a long time.

"I can feel the energy coming back between Brian and me onstage," he said. "I'm complementing Brian and freeing him up from carrying the entire load on this body of work. And I can go back to my original parts — which is quite a challenge because the music is in its original keys — and not clash with anybody else in the band."

Jardine said that he initially never imagined that the Beach Boys and their music would have such longevity.

"Not in the beginning," he said. "I thought it would be a one-hit deal and then I'd go back to dental school. But the Wilsons (Brian, Carl and Dennis) — along with Mike Love and Bruce Johnston — had a great blend and it was nice to be part of that blend."

And Jardine hinted that this might not be the last time he and Wilson get together.
"Frankly, we need all the rehearsal we can get at this point," said Jardine in reference to the upcoming tour dates. "But we'll see where it goes from here. We may do some other things together."

The night of the show, it became painfully evident early on that the fashion era of the Hawaiian shirt was over.
By my strictly unofficial count, out of about 1,400 people in the auditorium that evening — including the band — there were only five guys Hawaiian shirts in the building: Two Beach Boys onstage, which seems appropriate given that they're the Beach Boys, for crying out loud; and three guys in the crowd. Those who know me will be able to easily surmise who was wearing one of the three Hawaiian shirts in the crowd. It was kind of embarrassing . . . for The Blonde Accountant. Not for me, I love Hawaiian shirts.

For the record, though, there wasn't one beach ball being batted around by the crowd during the show. Really, how can we have a Brian Wilson concert

Dancing in My Underwear

— even by 2006 standards — without a plethora of multicolored Hawaiian shirts and no beach balls?

This was the fourth time I had seen Brian perform (twice at the Keswick and twice at the Mann Center for the Performing Arts in Philadelphia), all since 2000. I have seen the Beach Boys many times, the first being in 1980 in Cedar Rapids, Iowa. As I recall, the good folks of Cedar Rapids had no such fashion constraints on their Hawaiian shirts in 1980. In fact, Hawaiian shirts were considered formal wear in Iowa at that time, if memory serves me.

That energy that Jardine had talked about in his interview with me to preview this show was apparent at the Keswick concert. Brian was in fine voice and the band was incredible, as it has been the other times I have seen Wilson's performance. It was a great concert.

Wouldn't it be nice, I thought, if I had the opportunity to meet Brian and Al after the show?

And I was presented with that opportunity, thanks to the fine staff at the Keswick. Folks, you have to understand, in a profession like journalism where we are not supposed to be star-struck, meeting Brian Wilson and Al Jardine is like a baseball fan meeting Babe Ruth. Among the many thoughts rattling around my brain as I waited near the stage with a small group of people was, "Man, I really thought I had on the right shirt for this."

And then he appeared, the man himself, standing right in the middle of us. It will come as no surprise to Brian Wilson fans that, given his personal history and status as a rock star, he is not at ease with a crowd. The small group of people seemed aware of this and did not rush him. He posed for pictures and exchanged pleasantries with the adoring throng, but it seemed to me he was uncomfortable.

I stood beside him for a picture, but we did not converse, a hiccup in my normally aggressive reporter's nature. A brush with greatness and I couldn't think of anything to say. Boy, I just wasn't made for these times.

Al then appeared and I did have the opportunity to briefly chat with him.
Me: "Hi Al, Mike Morsch from Montgomery Newspapers. We did a phone interview last week."

Al: "Oh, hi Mike. Nice shirt."

No, he really didn't say that. Al was pleasant and not intimidated by the crowd. He posed for pictures, signed autographs and seemed genuinely moved and appreciative of the reception he got onstage and off.

And despite my fashion faux pas, it was indeed an evening filled with good vibrations.

Law & Order
Jill Hennessy
I didn't know she could sing

Life as a newspaper copy editor in the early to mid-1990s had both its positives and negatives. I started with Copley News in 1989 as a copy editor at The State Journal-Register in Springfield, Illinois, the capital city's daily newspaper, which had a circulation of around 70,000 at the time. It was considered the financial salad days of the industry, as everybody seemed to be making a boatload of money.

And for the first time in my career, I was drawing a reasonable salary for an honest day's work. It wasn't a boatload, but for the first time in my young career, I at least had a seat on the boat.

The parent company treated its employees fabulously and offered state-of-art facilities and equipment, overtime pay, Christmas bonuses and tons of respect. It was the best newspaper work environment that I had encountered up to that point and, although I didn't know it at the time, the best work environment that I would ever experience.

Copy editors are a unique group. Many journalists who start as reporters get tired of covering meetings, crime or business and opt to get out of the writing end and into the editing end of newspapers.

The copy editors — or "deskers" as they were called — are essentially the last line of eyes that look at the information a newspaper produces before it gets to the public. Copy editors do more than just proofread: they rewrite to improve sentence structure and flow; they make sure to distinguish the difference between State Street, State Avenue and State Road, as those very well could be three different locations in a city; they write headlines; back then, they laid out pages of the newspaper, determining which news went on

Dancing in My Underwear

which page; and in what many consider their best attribute, copy editors i general acted like the crankiest people on the planet.

They essentially have inferiority complexes, rarely if ever leave the offic and in many cases, could inhabit The Island of Misfit Toys qui comfortably.

When I walked into the State Journal-Register copy desk in January 1989, already had several years experience in newspapers but I was still pret much the rookie of the staff. It took me about a week to figure out that didn't know anything about anything and to question myself on just wh the hell I had been doing for the past seven years trying to build a career journalism.

Not only was the desk an experienced and grizzled group of vetera newspaper men and women, it was a cast of characters:

Eddie "White Shoes" Hamman — nicknamed thusly because he alwa violated the "No White Shoes after Labor Day" rule — was unique enoug to have a second nickname: The Dancer.

We called him The Dancer because between deadlines — we had two eac evening at 11 p.m. and 12:30 a.m. — he would engage in storytelling. Ar inevitably during his stories, as he stood by my desk and progressively g all wound up and excited, he couldn't contain himself and his feet wou start to tap and shuffle and move across the floor. Fred Astaire never glide across a room with more grace. By the time Eddie got done telling his stor he'd be 100 feet away from the copy desk and shouting the punchline bac to us.

Bob "Kitchen" Gonko was our dayside copy editor, so he wasn't arour during the evenings. His nickname originated because for years he wrote column called "Gonko's Kitchen," which was filled with cooking tips and recipes.

It was because of one of those columns that Bob would be forever cemented into copy desk lore, courtesy of one of his wiseass headline-writing brethren.

One Christmas season, Bob wrote a column on the baking of favorite treats, including the ever-popular holiday staple, fruitcake. The headline, which appeared right below Bob's picture on the column, read: "Say hello to a real fruitcake."

That's funny, although I'm not sure Bob thought so.

Jack Sutherland was a quiet and unassuming man, and by the time I got the opportunity to work with him, his career was on the downswing. The technology of the time, which was quite primitive compared to today's newspaper technology advances, had already passed Jack by even then. His role had been reduced essentially to just reading the obituaries, but they were the cleanest obits around. And obituaries are important to readers, so it was still a valuable contribution.

Maggie Boswell was our matron saint and the polar opposite of Jack Sutherland. Maggie was a chain-smoker and a loud talker. When I first joined the desk, smoking was still allowed in the newsroom, and there was a perpetual blue cloud of smoke hanging over Maggie's desk. But she could move copy and pages with the best of them, even if it wasn't pristine.

There were others on the desk – Ted Wolf, Gary Schieffer, Ron Correll, Daron Walker, Eric White – most of them strong personalities and journalists, and I enjoyed the nightly banter among us, taking it all in and trying to learn as much as I could.

Dancing in My Underwear

But the overwhelming experience I took away from being a desker for wh
would become 11 years was that we worked the worst hours, had the lea
appreciated job in the newsroom, missed a lot of holidays and got hom
really late every night – or real early the next morning, if you prefer.

I'd usually get home around 1:30 a.m. Unlike the rest of the 9-to-5 wor
that got home in time for dinner, I didn't eat my last meal of the day unt
around 2 a.m.

And for late-nighters, 2 a.m. was the bewitching hour for my favorite cab
TV show, "Law & Order," which already was in syndication. It was m
favorite show mostly because in that era, the early 1990s, it was the onl
real show on at that early hour. All the other channels showed on
infomercials.

So I became a fan of the show from 1993 through 1996 because that's whe
Canadian actress Jill Hennessy played assistant district attorney Clai
Kincaid - portrayed as an idealistic outspoken feminist and agnostic wh
becomes increasingly disillusioned with her job - on "Law & Order."

I was mesmerized by her acting and her incredibly good looks. OK, s
maybe it was her incredibly good looks more than anything else, but h
contribution to the show made it worth staying up until the wee hours of th
morning.

And then in 2009 – nearly 15 years after those late night/early mornir
hours watching her on "Law & Order" - I got an opportunity to intervie
Jill Hennessy, but not because of any television or movie role. It turned o
that she is a singer-songwriter who was releasing her debut CD ahead of
show scheduled at World Café Live in Philadelphia.

I didn't even know she could sing.

"Oh ya, I get that all the time, man," said Hennessy in a telephone interview from her home in Manhattan. "It's still sort of a new thing for the general public because I started to become known when I started to do 'Law & Order.'"

Apparently, she had been singing for quite some time by the time I talked to her. She began her show business career as a musician, singing on the streets of Toronto and later in the subways and coffeehouses of New York.

And now she was coming to Philadelphia in support of her first album, "Ghost in My Head."

"I was working with a couple of different bands at the time I auditioned for 'Law & Order.' I didn't even think I'd get that show, to be honest," she said. "Every acting job I've ever done I've always brought my guitar," said Hennessy, who is self-taught on the instrument. "It's just a great way for me to center myself, calm down and connect with other people."

During her years on "Law & Order," Hennessy said that she, other cast members and the crew would oftentimes hang out with each other when not filming and connect over music.

"On 'Law & Order,' we'd meet once a week - me and the crew and cast - and we'd just jam," she said. "We'd do bluegrass, contemporary stuff. We were just pulling out everything we could think of and just jamming. It was great."

Her character was written out of "Law & Order" at the end of the 1996 season by being killed in a car accident when her vehicle is hit by a drunken driver.

Dancing in My Underwear

Hennessy followed that with the successful and popular character Jordan Cavanaugh, the crime-solving medical examiner in "Crossing Jordan," which ran for six seasons from 2001 to 2007 on NBC.

But despite a series of stage and film roles in addition to her television work, Hennessy had decided in 2009 that it was time for her to concentrate on her music.

"I'd always wanted to write my own music and create my own album. But I didn't want to do it just to write an album. I wanted it to come from somewhere," she said. "And my dad has been pushing me since I was a kid to pursue the singing."

The end result is "Ghost in My Head," a series of emotional vignettes spun with fluid melodies and poignant musical reflections on love, loss, struggle and redemption.

"These are all stories from my past, things I'd wanted to get out for some time," said Hennessy. "Basically, these things tapped me on the shoulder and said, 'You know what, you gotta deal with this. You have to confront this. Let me out.' That's basically what this whole album is about."

The title track, "Ghost in My Head" is Hennessy's attempt to deal with something that she just didn't want to deal with.

"One of the best ways to cope with it was to write it down. So that song is a very literal account of dealing with a loss that I just didn't want to confront," she said. "Then after that, all these other stories came to my mind, things in my childhood or from friends of mine who had gone through some different kinds of brutal situations or ordeals. Writing music has helped me connect with people who I had become disconnected with."

An unexpected side benefit from the project was that it enabled Hennessy to involve her family. Husband Paolo Mastropietro produced the CD.

"We produced the CD from our kitchen table," said Hennessy. "I'm really thrilled with what we accomplished. It was kind of a benchmark in my life. It was something I never really thought I would get off my butt and conquer my fears to achieve."

As for what she was expecting at the World Café Live gig, Hennessy said it would be just Jill being Jill.

"I've got no stage persona," said Hennessy. "I wish I could get up there and be somebody cool and hip, but it ends up being just me, tuning my guitar and telling stories between songs.

"It's brilliantly terrifying because it's so exposing," she said. "But I really love it. I feel like I'm being more authentic than I've ever been and I'm really happy with that. It's been probably the most satisfying thing I've ever attempted."

As it turned out, the evening was as Hennessy had predicted, just Jill being Jill. Her voice is quite pleasing and her songs are thought-provoking.

The Blonde Accountant and I got to spend some time chatting with Hennessy and her husband before the show. She was pleasant, gracious and approachable. She talked with us for several minutes and posed for several pictures.

Hennessy is a talented actress and singer. I was as mesmerized by her in person as I had been 15 years earlier watching her on television in the middle of the night.

Barry Manilow
I right the wrongs, I right the wrongs

Barry Manilow was scheduled to have surgery on both his hips in late 2006. Seems as if the high-energy Las Vegas show that he was performing at the time had aggravated those hips of his.

I cannot begin to describe to you how little I would have cared about that particular bit of entertainment news in 2006 were it not for two big reasons: (1) The Blonde Accountant is a huge Barry Manilow fan, so by default, I am a huge Barry Manilow fan. Really. (2) And it's a good lead-in because in August 2006, she and I had recently returned from seeing that high-energy Las Vegas act and therefore considered ourselves eminently qualified to comment on Barry Manilow's hips. She more than I, of course.

See, that year for her birthday I thought it would be a nice present to take her to a Manilow concert, this despite the fact that I failed to grasp the concept that Barry was then performing year-round at the Las Vegas Hilton. And only at the Hilton. In Las Vegas. Nevada. Pacific Time Zone.

Las Vegas is a very long plane ride from Philadelphia for me, my wallet and my hips. And now I know why Barry Manilow has hip problems: He's carrying around a wallet that is waaaaayyyyy bigger than mine. And I know this because I paid $13.50 for a plastic cup of wine at the Las Vegas concert. And it wasn't even for me.

At this point I suppose I could hit you with that cute slogan about what happens in Vegas stays in Vegas. But I want everybody to know exactly what happened to me in Vegas that year, among the things of which included:
(1) I went to a Barry Manilow concert. And so did a bazillion members of the Barry Manilow International Fan Club (BMIFC), which just happened to

be having its annual convention the same weekend that The Blond
Accountant and I were there. Apparently we all were going hoppin' when
things were poppin'.

That was swell.

(2) The roulette tables and slot machines were not very friendly. I came and
I gave without taking, so they sent me away. Just dandy.

(3) Elvis might have left the building . . . and gone straight to the sidewalk
on Las Vegas Boulevard. That's just wrong. The King is dead, so I told the
imposter to go get a real job because, well . . . I right the wrongs, I right the
wrongs.

(4) Where were Frank, Dean and Sammy when I really needed them, babe? I
can't smile without them. I can't laugh and I can't sing. In fact, I'm finding it
hard to do anything.

The night of the concert the mood was electric. The Blonde Accountant was
positively giddy, as were all the members of the BMIFC.

The men in the audience were a little less so, I suspect, because none of us
could believe we were actually at a Barry Manilow concert and that we
couldn't afford to drink heavily with the alcohol prices such as they were.

We were seated stage left in the balcony, front row, which was a pretty good
vantage point in the intimate venue. I was seated next to The Blonde
Accountant on one side and a woman from Chicago on the other. I found out
that the Chicago Lady and her husband had been married for 27 years, and
the look on his face suggested that he, too, was a big Barry Manilow fan
just like me.

"Are you excited to be here?" I asked the lady.

152

"Oh my, yes! Are you?" she responded.

"Uh ... well ... hmmm. Ya, sure," I whispered, out of The Blonde Accountant's earshot.

So Barry performed for us on those bad hips. And as would be anticipated, The Blonde Accountant whooped it up. She and the Chicago Lady sang, danced, hooted, hollered, swooned, pirouetted and shook their booties like they were indeed in the hottest spot north of Havana.

My contribution? The usher had given us two of those little neon light sticks, so I waved one in the air after each song. I figured that was all Barry was going to get out of me.

In all honesty, I thought the show was very good, and I'm not just saying that to stay out of The Blonde Accountant's doghouse, although that wouldn't necessarily be a bad strategy. Barry puts on what I would consider to be a typical Las Vegas show - lots of glitz and glamour with plenty of cheese.

But he appeared to be very humble about his success and genuinely appreciative of the fan support he's received over the years.

Just more than a year later, I picked up the telephone in my office and heard the voice on the other end of the line say, "Mike, this is Barry Manilow."

I get a lot of phone calls at my office. Still, there are times when the voice on the other end of the line gives me pause because I never considered the possibility that I would ever talk to that person on the telephone.

This was one of those calls. I just wanted to respond, "Barry Manilow? No it's not! It's not really you, is it?"

Dancing in My Underwear

But I didn't say that. It really was Barry Manilow. I was going to do an interview with him to preview his upcoming show at what was then known as the Wachovia Center in the sports complex in South Philadelphia.

"Philadelphia was always very kind to me," said Manilow on getting his start in the city more than 30 years ago. "They didn't run out for orange juice on me like I thought they would. And when I came back the next year, they were very kind. I really broke out in Philly."

Indeed. And given what's happened to Manilow's career since he started in Philadelphia, it was unlikely that no matter how much orange juice was available, the fans in the Philadelphia area weren't likely to run out on one of their favorite sons when he opened his what was a highly anticipated tour in September 2007 to promote his latest album, "The Greatest Songs of the Seventies.

And despite all the success he had with his Las Vegas show over a several-year period – which The Blonde Accountant and I had witnessed while we were there the year before - and the throngs of adoring fans he's accumulated just about everywhere, Manilow is still incredulous about the whole ride.

"I had no idea that this [a successful music career] would ever happen to me," said Manilow in the telephone interview. "I was just an obnoxious songwriter. When I got out on my own, I was just shocked, shocked! thought it would be over after every record."

Let the record show that it's still not over, at least, it wasn't in 2007.

Rolling Stone magazine had proclaimed Manilow "The Showman of Our Generation." The 2007 album was the 60th album of his career, which has encompassed nearly every arena of music, including performing composing, arranging and producing.

He's in the Songwriters Hall of Fame. Industry charts ranked him at the time as the undisputed number one adult contemporary artists of all time, with record sales exceeding 65 million worldwide. He's won a Grammy, two Emmys, several Tony awards and an Oscar nomination.

And he got his start right there in Philadelphia. After teaming up with Bette Midler as her music director, arranger and pianist in 1972, Manilow recorded his first solo album. Surrounding the release of the now-memorable and classic "Mandy" two years later, Manilow performed six of his first seven solo performances at Philadelphia's Bijou Café in March 1974.

"The Seventies was a very confusing era for me," said Manilow. "It was the best of times, it was the worst of times. It was not my favorite decade, but it was an exciting decade. I just didn't understand what the people liked about me. I was a musician, not a performer."

"Mandy" launched a career of 25 consecutive top 40 hits, including "Even Now," "This One's for You," "Weekend in New England," "I Write the Songs" and "Tryin' to Get That Feeling Again."

In 1978, five of Manilow's albums were on the charts simultaneously, a record rivaled only by Frank Sinatra and Johnny Mathis.

"The Greatest Songs of the Seventies" was the next release in a best-selling series of tribute albums of popular music and followed Manilow's successful "The Greatest Songs of the Fifties" and "The Greatest Songs of the Sixties."

Among the songs covered on the record are the Beatles' "The Long and Winding Road," Elton John's "Sorry Seems to Be the Hardest Word," Simon and Garfunkel's "Bridge Over Troubled Waters," the Hollies' "He

Dancing in My Underwear

Ain't Heavy, He's My Brother," The Carpenters' "Close to You" and Albert Hammond's "It Never Rains in Southern California."

Also included in the two-disc set are six stripped-down acoustic versions of some of Manilow's most endearing hits, including "Mandy," "I Write the Songs," "Even Now," "Looks Like We Made It," "Weekend in New England" and "Copacabana."

"It's going to be a great show," said Manilow of the Wachovia Center appearance. "I hope the fans in Philadelphia are still excited to see me because I'll be excited to see them."

Oh, we were.

Manilow was so tickled by the reception he received from the Philly fans that night that he promised to buy a trip to Bermuda for all those in attendance.

It may have been a trip to the Bahamas. I couldn't tell. There was so much commotion by the rush of people calling their travel agents that I wasn't sure if he said Bermuda or the Bahamas.

Nevertheless, I just happened to be looking for a honeymoon destination at that point – The Blonde Accountant and I were scheduled to get married month later - and either Bermuda or the Bahamas would have been perfectly okie dokie with me. And if Barry was promising to foot the bill, then I was certainly going to be a Barry Manilow fan for the evening. I know, I know for a guy who grew up with the Beach Boys as well as a fair amount of country music, it's a miracle, a true-blue spectacle - a miracle come true. Woo. Or maybe woo, pardner.

I just wish I would have known in 2006 that Barry's tour schedule was going to allow him to get out of Las Vegas. Jeez, the guy couldn't have

156

come to Philly a year earlier and saved me airfare, hotel fees and contributions to the Las Vegas roulette tables? I suppose since he was now offering to pay for the Bermuda/Bahamas trip, I could have overlooked that inconvenience.

And although this was only my second Barry concert, I was beginning to pick up the Manilow Fan Tendencies. For this performance, I observed:
(1) It was Hawaiian Shirt Night at the Barry Manilow Concert. Unfortunately, I did not get the memo. You may recall my one-time fondness for Hawaiian shirts. However, The Blonde Accountant does not share that same fondness for island outerwear, and I have exactly zero Hawaiian shirts left in my closet. I consider this a hole in my wardrobe. She considers that concept a hole in my head.

But the fact that her guy Barry was about to perform and she may have been distracted by the excitement of the moment ... I thought it an opportune time to try and diversify the style of shirts in my closet.

Me: "Hey, look at all the guys wearing Hawaiian shirts here tonight."

TBA: "No."

Me: "But, I like Hawaiian shirts. They are comfortable and attractive ...."

TBA: "No."

Me: "I'll bet Barry Manilow likes Hawaiian shirts."
TBA: "Stop it."

(2) It was Show Your Cleavage Night for Women at the Barry Manilow Concert. Uh ... hmmm ... well ... ahem. Fortunately, The Blonde Accountant got that memo. That may be the biggest reason right there for me to become more of a Barry Manilow fan.

Dancing in My Underwear

(3) Manilow fans like neon green glow sticks. In fact, along with tick
takers, souvenir sales people, popcorn vendors and the like, the Glow Stic
Guy was among the more popular concert employees. I've never seen adul
go so ga-ga over a glow stick, but the same thing happened with the La
Vegas glow sticks a year earlier. Why, I saved mine from the Philly sho
and put it in the freezer when I got home. And I have no idea why.

(4) I know all the words to "Mandy" and "I Write the Songs." I did n
realize this. But as a card-carrying member of the Seventies Preservatic
Society, this is not an entirely huge surprise. What is a surprise is that
actually like those songs more now than I did in the 1970s. I may need to l
examined by a professional psychiatric evaluator to determine the reason f
that.

(5) Throughout the whole concert, The Blonde Accountant screamed to tl
point where she lost her voice. And a woman behind me kept shoutin
"Wow! Wow! Wow!" during the whole performance. I assume that mear
she was wowed by Barry. Unfortunately, that woman did not lose her voice

See, guys, I think going to a Barry Manilow concert has turned into quite a
attractive proposal for us men, whether or not you like the man's music. W
get to wear our Hawaiian shirts (well, most of you do), we get inundate
with cleavage and we get glow sticks to take home to put in the freezer.

If you ask Barry, I'm sure he would agree: Looks like we made it.

A Bronx Tale
Chazz Palminteri
How lucky can one guy be?

There's an absolutely hilarious scene in the 1993 film "A Bronx Tale" that makes the movie one of my favorite films of all time.

Sonny, a New York neighborhood mob boss, is with his crew in the basement of a bar named the "Chez Bippy," which serves as Sonny's headquarters and where he conducts all neighborhood business.

Many of the goodfellas in the story have those wonderfully creative mob nicknames — Jimmy Whispers (Sonny's main man; he was "Whispers" because everything was a secret to him), Bobby Bars (spent half his life behind them), Tony Toupee (because of his lousy hairpiece), Eddie Mush (a degenerate gambler and the world's biggest loser; everything he touched turned to mush), JoJo the Whale (if you stared long enough, you'd see him get fatter by the hour; legend has it that his shadow once killed a dog) and Frankie Coffeecake (his face looked like a Drake's coffeecake; he was tough to look at).

The degenerate wannabe wiseguys are all engaged in a high-stakes craps game, with Sonny right in the middle, dominating everything.

A 9-year-old kid named Calogero — who Sonny affectionately calls "C" — is working the game, serving drinks. The kid's dad is a law-abiding bus driver who doesn't want his son hanging around the criminal elements associated with Sonny. But the mob boss has taken a liking to the kid.

To improve his luck in the craps game, Sonny asks the kid to throw the dice for him. But before the kid tosses the dice, Sonny continues to try to improve his odds through a series of superstitious moves that culminate in

Dancing in My Underwear

Eddie Mush, JoJo the Whale and Frankie Coffeecake all being put in the small basement bathroom so as to not jinx the kid.

The youngster makes 11 passes with the dice without crapping out and makes Sonny a pile of money. As the winning streak begins, we hear Dean Martin's version of "Ain't That a Kick in the Head" as the music background for the kid's – and Sonny's – good fortune.

It's the best scene in a movie full of best scenes.

"A Bronx Tale" is essentially the life story of actor Chazz Palminteri, who first performed it as a one-man stage play. Robert De Niro — ya, *the* Robert De Niro — saw the show and wanted to make it into a movie. Palminteri agreed, but only if he could write the screenplay and star in the movie.

It was an offer that De Niro couldn't refuse.

So Palminteri starred as Sonny the mob boss, with De Niro — in his directing debut as well — starring as the kid's law-abiding, working-man bus driver father.

Not only do I love this movie, but I also love its soundtrack, which features a wonderful street corner a capella doo-wop group called Cool Change singing the title song "The Streets of the Bronx," which serves as both the opening and the closing of the film.

When it was time for The Blonde Accountant and me to plan our wedding in 2007, we, along with her children, Kaitie and Kevin, all sat down one evening and made what turned out to be a wonderful family memory by taking a few hours to pick out all the songs that we wanted played on our special day.

I had one specific contribution that I wanted to make. There is a point at most weddings where the ceremony has been completed and everyone has been through the receiving line. Sometimes, there are more pictures taken of the bride and groom,
which gives the guests an opportunity to make their way to the reception.
When it's time to start the reception, someone will grab a microphone – in our case it was the deejay hired for the event – and make a big production out of presenting the newly married couple to the crowd: "Ladies and gentlemen, Mr. and Mrs. Mike Morsch!"

At that point in our special day, I wanted to hear Dean Martin's version of "Ain't That a Kick in the Head" – the same song played during the fabulous dice game scene in "A Bronx Tale" – because the opening line of that song is: "How lucky can one guy be? I kissed her and she kissed me . . . ."

A year later, in October 2008, I was on the phone with Chazz Palminteri. He was bringing his one-man stage play of "A Bronx Tale" to the Merriam Theater in Philadelphia and I was interviewing him for a preview story.

"That's exactly how the craps games were. They were down in the hole, down in the basement," said Palminteri. "But as far as throwing them in the bathroom, that only happened once and I thought it was a funny thing and never forgot it. When we would watch a game, Eddie Mush would be there – he was a jinx – and we'd say 'Throw Mush in the bathroom!' I thought it would be a funny thing to put in the craps game. So there it was.

"That was the real Eddie Mush in the movie. He was terrific. That was Bob's [De Niro] idea to put him there. When I introduced him to Bob, he said, 'Where are we going to get somebody to play him? Forget it; let him do it."

Dancing in My Underwear

Legend has it that Eddie Mush – whose real name was Eddie Montanaro
was such a jinx that the first day she showed up for filming on the movie .
it rained.

The thrust of the movie, however, centered around something that happen
to Palminteri when he was 9 years old. His father had helped train a 17-yea
old boxer who had a tremendous amount of potential, only to make a b
decision with drugs that ended his life. Because of that, Palminteri's fath
wanted to make sure his young son didn't fall into the same trap. So he ga
his boy a card on which was written some sage advice: "The saddest thing
life is wasted talent."

And Palminteri listened. Not only that, he used that advice as the premi
for "A Bronx Tale," the story about a young boy's rough childhood and t
people he encountered in a 1960s-era Bronx neighborhood.

Palminteri had already experienced success with the story off-Broadway a
in the initial Broadway run of "A Bronx Tale." He was back again, playir
18 different characters in the one-man production.

"After all these years, people just constantly talk about that movie and t
show," said Palminteri in the telephone interview from San Francisco whe
he was at the time in the midst of a successful run there of "A Bronx Tale
"I hear so many times how it's helped people. I just said, 'You know, there
a whole new generation of people who never really saw the show,' and
decided to do it one more time. And it's been a wonderful thing."

Palminteri said "A Bronx Tale" is about 75 percent autobiographical. T
story is about a young boy who, while sitting on the stoop outside h
parents' Bronx apartment, witnesses a murder committed by t
neighborhood mob boss. The boy refuses to rat out the mob boss to t
police, and the mob boss takes the youngster under his wing. In real lif
Palminteri did actually witness the murder as a young boy.

The boy's father, a law-abiding bus driver, tries to teach his son that the working man is the "real tough guy." An internal struggle ensues within the boy as he tries to make the right decisions in life, given the conflicting influences of his father and the mob boss.

"As bad as Sonny was, Sonny was a good guy," said Palminteri. "He constantly told you to do the right thing, to go to college. But because of who he was, you couldn't help be influenced by him. He didn't want this boy to do what he did; he wanted the boy to do the right thing. He treated the boy like his own son. Sonny was lonely; he was a lonely character.

"The stage show is even more powerful than the movie," said Palminteri. "It's a whole different experience and people who come to see it realize that. It's a much more visceral experience.

"I am the little boy, so onstage that is very powerful," he said. "It reaches out and grabs you by the throat. The play is also much funnier than the movie because I was able to put more characters in the play that I couldn't put in the movie."

Palminteri has appeared in more than 50 films, including "The Usual Suspects," "Analyze This," "Hurley Burley," "Mulholland Falls" and Woody Allen's 1994 film, "Bullets over Broadway," for which Palminteri was nominated for the Academy Award as best supporting actor.

He has directed the HBO series "Oz," and Showtime's "Women vs. Men," as well as the feature film "Noel," starring Susan Sarandon, Penelope Cruz and Robin Williams. He also was seen on the New York stage in the play "The Resistible Rise of Arturo Ui," starring Al Pacino, John Goodman and Steve Buscemi.

But back in 1989, he had only his one-man stage production of "A Bronx Tale" and about $200 in the bank. Studios, producers and directors all

wanted to make a film version of the play, but none wanted him in a starrir
role.

Then Robert De Niro came to see the show and liked it so much that l
decided to make it his film directorial debut.

"It was difficult to turn down a million bucks when I had only $200 in tl
bank," said Palminteri. "Basically, none of the people who wanted to mak
it a film would guarantee me the role of Sonny. But Bob was the perfe
director and guaranteed I would play the part and write the screenpla
which I wanted."

I love it when somebody knows Robert De Niro well enough to refer to hii
as "Bob."

"I enjoyed writing the screenplay very much," said Palminteri. "For me,
love my acting but I really enjoy my writing. I think actors come and go b
the writing stays forever."

Palminteri admitted that the stage production is physically demanding, wh
with him playing all 18 characters. But for him, it's much more.

"You gotta fly," he said of being the 18 different characters onstage. "B
you know what, when I do it - I hate to sound like this because some peopl
they laugh - it's a spiritual thing. I just feel I'm this other thing, this channe
I get these feelings and I just fly across the stage when I do it. I'm tellir
you, it's from another place. It's just weird."

In an odd and unfortunate twist of fate, the actor who played the teenage bc
in the film version of "A Bronx Tale," Lillo Brancato Jr., ended up in jai
charged with second-degree murder for his role in a Bronx burglary th
ended up with the death of an off-duty police officer.

"I hold Lillo up there as the poster boy for the movie," said Palminteri. "Here this young boy is in the quintessential movie about not wasting your life and that's exactly what he does.

"It broke my heart for the police officer and his family. Here is a man trying to do his duty and he ends up getting killed," he said. "When I go talk to young kids, I go, 'Look, here is this young boy who had all this talent and he totally wasted it. You know why? Because he made the wrong choices.'"

Fortunately for Palminteri, his father, who had died six months before my interview at the age of 90, got to see his son make the right choices and build a successful career.

"When I get to the end of the play, he's there," said Paminteri of his father. "When I'm hugging and talking to the father in the story, he's there. He was a great man. And the father's influence in the play is much bigger than in the movie."

Palminteri said at the time he was looking forward to bringing "A Bronx Tale" to Philadelphia.

"The amazing thing [about this story] is that you see kids from 12 years old to people in their 80s standing up at the end," he said. "It just resonates with everyone. It's one of those things that's like lightning in a bottle. It hits all the ages and people just right.

"I've never performed in Philly, but I love the city," he said. "I'm really looking forward to going there, going to Tony Luke's and having a cheesesteak. I know those guys. They're great guys and they got great cheesesteaks."

And I got to talk to the guy – Chazz Palminteri, who wrote and starred in one of my favorite scenes of one of my most favorite movies of all time. A guy who gets to call Robert De Niro – who has starred in two of my other favorite movies of all-time, "Goodfellas" and "Godfather II" – by the much more informal first name of "Bob."

Ain't that a kick in the head? Really, how lucky can one guy be?

Hall & Oates
Daryl Hall
The smile that lives forever

When it was time for The Blonde Accountant and I to walk down the aisle in October 2007, selecting the music for our big day became a family affair, just like we wanted it to be.

And we wanted her kids to be involved. So we sat down one evening with a collection of CDs and started brainstorming. Although a majority of the music would be chosen by the bride and groom – we were, after all, footing the bill for this hootenanny – we wanted the kids, Katie, who was 12 at the time and Kevin, who was 10 at the time, to contribute some of their favorite and special songs to help mark the event. Because it was the second marriage for both of us, we thought it was something important and meaningful that we could share as a new family.

Gathered in the family room one evening, it must have taken us three or four hours to choose the entire list of songs for the wedding day. Someone would throw out a suggestion, we'd see if we had the song, and if so, we'd pop it into the CD player and give it a test run for everybody to hear. The songs that made the cut were put onto a master list that we would give to the DJ hired to handle the music that day. Those songs that didn't make the cut were soon forgotten.

When it was complete, our list reflected what each of us wanted to contribute to the proceedings. And not surprisingly, it broke across generational lines.

Kevin chose "You'll Be in My Heart" and "Son of Man," both by Phil Collins.

Dancing in My Underwear

Kaitie selected "Love Just Is" by Hilary Duff and "When You Really Lov
Someone" by Alicia Keyes.

The Blonde Accountant – who got to choose whatever she wanted to dam
well choose because there wouldn't be anybody happy unless the bride wa
happy – had an eclectic mix:
"Sunday Mornings" by Maroon 5.
"You Raise Me Up" by Josh Groban.
"Moondance" by Van Morrison.
"Truly, Madly, Deeply" by Savage Garden.
"Everything" by Michael Buble.
"Because You Love Me" by Celine Dion.
"Could It Be Magic" by Barry Manilow.
"You're the Inspiration" by Chicago.
"The Way You Look Tonight" by Rod Stewart.
"Better When We're Together" by Jack Johnson.
And "How Sweet It Is (To Be Loved by You) and "You've Got a Friend" t
James Taylor.

And then it was the old guy's contributions, some of which actual
overlapped with the bride, eight years his junior. My list included:
"Fun, Fun, Fun" by the Beach Boys.
"How Deep Is Your Love" by the BeeGees.
'Wonderful World" by Louis Armstrong.
"Paper Doll" by the Mills Brothers.
"Ain't That a Kick in the Head" by Dean Martin.
"Happy Together" by theTurtles.
"Brown-Eyed Girl" by Van Morrison.
"You're Beautiful" by James Blunt.

But when it came to choosing what song we would dance our first dance
as husband and wife, we had narrowed it down to three finalalists: "Go

Bless the Broken Road" by Rascal Flatts; "More Than Love" by Los Lonely Boys; and "Sara Smile" by Hall and Oates.

Ah, "Sara Smile." I had grown up with the music of Daryl Hall and John Oates, long before I knew I would someday be moving to the Philadelphia area and into the same county where both of them grew up.

"Sara Smile" was released in January 1976 as a single off the self-titled album "Daryl Hall & John Oates." It was the "Philly soul" duo's first Top 10 hit, reaching No. 4 on the Billboard charts that year. Co-written by both Daryl and John, it's a song that was actually about Hall's girlfriend at the time, Sara Allen. That relationship lasted nearly 30 years, ending in 2001.

I was so taken by the song "Sara Smile" that when my first daughter, Kiley Brianna, was born in 1988, 12 years after the song's release, I wanted to name her Sara Smile Morsch. But my wife at the time had grown up with a girl named Sara whom she didn't particularly like, so there was no way I was going to have a daughter named Sara.

Still, it's a great song and has been for a long time.

And 33 years after its release, I was on the phone with Daryl Hall.

Hall admitted that even after all these years together, he and John Oates never have a bad show in Philadelphia. Hey, they're both local guys who made it big, so it's no real surprise they're always well received on their home turf and have been for quite some time.

The reason for this interview was to talk about the closing and subsequent demolition of the legendary Spectrum, located in the sports complex in South Philly.

Dancing in My Underwear

Hall & Oates were the next-to-last group scheduled to perform on October 23, 2009, as part of the Final Farewell Concert Series at the historic Spectrum (Pearl Jam had the final four dates), which closed October 31 and was demolished soon thereafter.

It was the seventh time that Hall & Oates had played the Spectrum — the first time was December 12, 1977 — and for this show, many of the tickets were rolled back to $4, $5 and $6 per seat, just as they were for the Quaker City Jazz Festival, the first-ever event at the Spectrum in 1967.

It's Hall & Oates — and at those prices. Needless to say, the concert sold out immediately.

"It's one of those ends of an era," said Hall in a telephone interview from his home in upstate New York. "For anybody that ever worked in Philadelphia, be it in sports or certainly music, the Spectrum is part of my history and all of our history."

That history was on full display in the duo's latest project at the time, the just-released "Do What You Want, Be What You Are," a four-CD box set that includes 74 songs from 1966 through 2009, including 16 previously unreleased tracks.

"I learned a lot, and some things that I didn't know," said Hall, of putting the box set together. "Usually after I finish a piece of music, I don't really pay much attention to it after that other than to play it live.

"But for the first time, really, the project forced me to sit down and listen to my entire musical life, just in one big gulp. I really heard, I think, what I do individually and what I do with John and the band," he said.

Hall said that among the things he heard for the first time was the progression and evolution of what Hall & Oates was in the beginning and what the duo became.

"The roads we took, the dead ends that we hit and the breakthroughs that we had. All of those things," said Hall. "It sort of all came together in my head to make me realize what it was that defines my music. It's really a rare thing. It was an eye-opener . . . an ear-opener, really."

These days, Hall & Oates still tour together occasionally, although both have pursued solo projects for several years. One of those projects for Hall has been something called "Live from Daryl's House," an innovative monthly Internet webcast that features Hall playing along with some friends and colleagues in an intimate setting.

"Every show is just an amazing experience because you never know what's going to happen," said Hall. "You throw my band and friends together with another person or people and anything can happen. It's just sort of an on-your-toes musical experience. I like a challenge and so does my band."

As for the Philly music scene in 2009, Hall said it remained as vibrant and tough then as it had been when he tackled it in the 1960s.

"It's something in the water, I don't know," he said. "There is something in a regional scene like Philadelphia that has the ability to stay vibrant. What I'm glad of is that it's still a regional thing. There is a different way of listening and looking at music in the Philly area that they don't do in other places."

As for his more than 40-year partnership with Oates, Hall said that the Philly music scene toughened them up and thickened their skin. "It was a hard road and I think we learned early on how to be relentless," he said.

Dancing in My Underwear

"As far as me and John working together, I think it has a lot to do with our differences and the fact that we don't really spend a lot of time together anymore," said Hall. "We live separate lives and we think of ourselves as two individuals who happen to have shared various projects over the years.

"Our touring company is called 'Two-Headed Monster' . . . that's what we're not."

Hall, a Pottstown native who graduated from Owen J. Roberts High School, said he still has family in the suburban Philadelphia counties.

"It was a great place to grow up. But it's changed a lot, as everybody knows," he said. "When I was a kid, Pottstown was a small town. It was farmland and great old houses, which I love. It's a great region and I'm really proud to come from there."

And now, I'm from there and have been for the past 12 years. Who knew that I'd end up living the same place where the guys who wrote "Sara Smile" grew up? Certainly not I.

Oh yeh, "Sara Smile." As much as The Blonde Accountant and I love that song, it wasn't the one played for our first dance at the wedding.

That honor went to Los Lonely Boys and the group's "More Than Love."

Wynonna Judd

I'm smelling good for you and not her

Sometimes the memorable story comes after the interview. Such was the case with Wynonna Judd in December 2007.

Judd was taking her Top 10 Billboard country album "A Classic Christmas" — which was released in October 2006 — on the road for her first-ever Christmas tour, and the Keswick Theatre in Glenside, Pa., was one stop in an 18-city tour.

During a telephone interview from her home just outside of Nashville, Wynonna was funny, witty, charming and honest.

"I'm not going to dress my band members up like elves or anything like that," she said about the Christmas tour, a sentiment that surely elicited a sigh of relief from the band.

At the time, Wynonna said she was starting anew professionally, despite the physical challenges of touring.

"I think at this age I'm starting to get it. I'm grateful in a way that comes with experience and wisdom. But I don't get tired of the people and the music," she said. "Sometimes I think, 'If I have to tease my hair just one more time, I'm going to call Dolly and ask her where she gets her wigs.' "

She said that this particular tour was about intimacy, fellowship and taking chances. And the intimacy of the Keswick played directly into what Wynonna was seeking to achieve during the tour.

173

Dancing in My Underwear

"When you play big stadiums, there is a lot of audience hysteria," she said. "For me it gets to be about the noise level. It's definitely a rush, but it can get overwhelming.

"It's hard to be emotionally transparent in a large group. If we're not to careful, we become caricatures of ourselves."

Not so with that tour.

"We can be ourselves. We can get into the audience and see someor crying, someone laughing. People in the audience have started to talk to m now."

Wynonna related one anecdote about going into the audience and bein handed a cell phone by a fan. The fan said that it was her mother on the lin and that the mother was dying of cancer.

"I had to take a chance during that concert and take the phone. The woma on the line will never forget that," said Wynonna.

The tour was also self-serving for Wynonna on a couple of levels. First, s brought along her musical mentor and what she called her "spiritual fathe — Don Potter, who was in the band with Wynonna and her mother Naon during the duo's run as the Judds.

From 1984 through 1991, the mother-daughter combo became one of th most celebrated groups in country music, selling more than 20 millic records and winning more than 60 industry awards including fi Grammies, nine CMAs and eight Billboard music awards. By 1989 th were one of the top-grossing acts in America selling more concert ticke that year than every other band except the Grateful Dead and the Rollir Stones.

Secondly, the tour came at an opportune time in Wynonna's personal life. While not elaborating on it, she suggested that it had gone through some bumps.

Published reports at the time revealed that in March 2006, Wynonna had filed for divorce from her husband of more than three years, Dan Roach, after Roach was indicted in Tennessee on three charges of aggravated sexual battery against a minor under the age of 13. And she had already at the time battled a well-publicized eating disorder as well.

"It's [the tour] saving my life personally," she said. "I'm doing it to keep myself busy and be around the people and music that I love. Thank you, God, for saving my life at a difficult time."

Despite that, Wynonna said her voice had held up well over the years.

"It's beyond anything I can describe," she said. "It's gotten deeper and wider and more soulful. I think that comes from wisdom and the experience of being on the road. It's not arrogance, it's confidence."

A few weeks after the interview, The Blonde Accountant and I had made plans to attend the show. See, I'm a little bit country and she's not. So getting her to attend a Wynonna concert was a pretty big score for me.

And then I got an email from Wynonna's publicist that read: "Wynonna personally asked to see you backstage." There was no further explanation.

Hmmm. Well, I certainly needed to tell The Blonde Accountant about this development.

"You know, Wynonna asked to see me personally before the show," I said to The Blonde Accountant.

Dancing in My Underwear

"She's pretty good-looking. I don't know if I should let you go backstage to see her or not without me," she said.

"But Wynonna didn't ask to see you backstage," I said.

Oh boy. For those of you who have been married, this is not the correct way to handle this situation.

The opportunity to meet Wynonna had apparently clouded my judgment at that point in the conversation, so much so that I had momentarily forgotten every single dadgummed thing I ever learned in Man School with that insensitive wisecrack. Consequently, there was a distinct possibility that I would spend the next three days trying to pull a Wynonna CD out of my ear.

The day of the performance, The Blonde Accountant and I were sharing bathroom time in preparation for our night out. Now occasionally, I am a cologne guy, but usually not every day and only when I dress up for special occasions.

As I began to spritz on a little cologne, I noticed in the bathroom mirror that The Blonde Accountant's eyes darted toward me and it was immediately clear — to me, at least — that as long as I still had one good ear left, that it might be a good idea to dispel any wrong notions that I was spritzing for some nefarious reason.

"I'm not putting this cologne on for Wynonna!" I shouted into the image in the mirror.

Of course, she wasn't thinking that at all, but rather was wondering if after I spritzed on the cologne whether I was going to be inclined to address the issue of some unruly nose hair before I went out in public.

Oh. Sorry, my bad.

When we arrived that evening at the Keswick Theatre, there were indeed two backstage passes waiting for us, which suggested that I wasn't the only one Wynonna wanted to see backstage after all. We followed the instructions on the passes and arrived at the designated area at the appointed time.

Moments before the show was to begin, we were escorted backstage to see Wynonna.

"Are you the one?" asked Wynonna as she extended her hand.

"I'm the one," I responded, not knowing what I was one of. "This is my wife, Judy," I said, and it was all I could do to not blurt out, "And I'm smelling good for her and not you!"

That likely would have been more information than Wynonna wanted to know, but it may have been prudent since we were in a venue where Wynonna CDs were readily available and within reach.

We chatted for a few moments about life, kids and our interview, and then took some pictures. I gave Wynonna a copy of the story I had written and she said she hadn't yet read it but would read it later.

I still don't know why she wanted to see me backstage. There would have been no way for her to know how good I smelled over the phone.

Wynonna's a big-time entertainer with big-time pipes. She was as engaging and sincere with the audience during the performance as she was with us backstage prior to it. And she gave a spirited performance, full of sassiness and heart.

Dancing in My Underwear

And me — well, it wasn't a waste of cologne after all, as I came out smelling pretty good when it was all said and done — I got to go home with the real star of the evening.

And ever since then, whenever The Blonde Accountant and I are sharing the bathroom getting ready to go out for a night on the town and I reach for the cologne, she gives me the eye.

My response is always the same: "Hey, you never know. We may see Wynonna tonight."

The Beach Boys
Jeffrey Foskett
McGuinn and McGuire couldn't get no higher
. . . and neither could I

The most perspective I've ever gotten on Brian Wilson didn't come in an interview with Brian himself, or with the other surviving members of the Beach Boys – Mike Love, Al Jardine or Bruce Johnston.

It came from Jeffrey Foskett. Longtime Brian Wilson fans will recognize Foskett and his work. He serves as Wilson's musical director, plays guitar and sings — flawlessly and beautifully — all the parts of songs that Brian's voice can no longer accommodate.

Aside from the Beach Boys themselves, Foskett has had a front-row seat for the part of rock and roll history that is the Beach Boys and Brian Wilson.

And in 2009, in advance of yet another Brian Wilson concert at the Keswick Theatre in Glenside, Pa., I talked with Foskett at length about Brian and the Beach Boys.

He related a story about the first time he met Brian. On his 20th birthday, Foskett walked up to the front door of Brian's house, knocked on the door and asked to see Brian. Not only was he let in, but Foskett and Wilson ended up in the rock and roll icon's music room.

"He was actually very lucid," said Foskett in a telephone interview as he recalled his first meeting in 1976 with the music legend. "He wasn't in good physical shape. But he wasn't drugged out, he wasn't drunk, he wasn't like any of the stories you may have heard going around at that time. That wasn't my experience at all."

Dancing in My Underwear

Foskett noticed Wilson's bass guitar up against the wall in a corner of the music room.

"I thought, 'Well, that has to be the bass that was played on all the [Beach Boys] albums and that he played onstage at the Hollywood Bowl.'

"I asked him if I could play it and he said yes. So I picked it up and played it and he sat down at the piano and we jammed a little bit. It was very fun."

And that essentially was the beginning of a more than 30-year relationship among Foskett, the Beach Boys and Brian Wilson that exists to this day.

"It's been an interesting ride," said Foskett. "People say they're big Beach Boys fans and I'm sure they are. But I was a huge, huge, huge Beach Boys fan."

After that initial meeting, Foskett stayed in touch with Brian. In the late 1970s, some of Foskett's friends were in the band Papa Doo Run Run which was then the house band in Disneyland in Anaheim, Calif.

Brian liked Papa Doo Run Run and would occasionally show up at the Disneyland gig and sit in with the band. Foskett's buddies would give him a heads up when Brian was going to show up, so the two saw each other periodically.

Then in the early 1980s, Carl Wilson of the Beach Boys – Brian's younger brother - decided to try a solo career, and the band was looking for a voice to replace Carl. Beach Boys frontman Mike Love had heard Foskett perform with the band Reverie and Love actually was the one who hired Foskett to join the Beach Boys.

"The reason Carl was so frustrated with the Beach Boys that he left to do solo career was that he wanted to get things back to a good-sounding touring band that was a great show to go to," said Foskett. "Over the years they had gone from five or six singers down to maybe four guys who were singing all the time. So they were manipulating the vocal parts to accommodate that. Carl thought they should go back to doing the original parts."

Carl Wilson came back to the Beach Boys a year later, and Foskett thought his own time with the band was over.

"But Carl really liked the way that I sang — it wasn't so much my guitar playing — and he said, 'You're a valuable asset.'"

So Foskett stayed with the Beach Boys, touring through 1990 and singing all of Brian's falsetto parts on all those famous Beach Boys tunes.

Foskett eventually left the Beach Boys to pursue a solo career for several years, where he experienced great overseas success, especially in New Zealand and Japan. Foskett has released more than a dozen solo CDs, including "Through My Window," which has been called "The best Beach Boys album they never recorded."

Then in the mid-1990s, Foskett and Brian Wilson's paths crossed again, this time at the wedding of a mutual friend.

"I was shocked because Brian was sitting there with his wife, Melinda, and everybody was afraid to go up and talk to him," said Foskett. "It's pretty intimidating when you think about it. It's Brian Wilson. But I wasn't intimidated because we were friends.

"So I just went up and sat down at the table and said, 'Hey, man, I hear you're working on a new record and I'd love to be involved. And he said, 'Hey, I think you're on to something.'"

Dancing in My Underwear

The album was Wilson's fourth solo album, "Imagination," which was released in 1998. And Foskett has been with Wilson ever since, getting an up-close-and-personal look at the genius that is Brian Wilson.

"Maybe Mozart deserved it and maybe Brian," said Foskett in reference to Wilson being tagged with the "genius" label. "Honestly, that's about it. If you want to call these other guys musical geniuses because they write one good song, I don't think that is appropriate. But in Brian's case, I think that it's certainly appropriate."

To illustrate his point, Foskett tells a story in reference to Wilson's famous "Pet Sounds" album. When Wilson decided in 2006 to do a tour surrounding the 40th anniversary of the landmark album's release in 1966, he and Foskett were discussing the song "I Just Wasn't Made for These Times."

"I said, 'Brian, that's so far out, those string parts. What did those guys [the musicians] say when you were recording it [the original in 1966]?'

"He said, 'I remember it well. I had some guys from the L.A. Philharmonic come in and play. They looked at me, looked at the music, heard the track and said, "What the hell is this? These parts are never going to work."

"That was a classically trained musician looking at it from his formal musical education," said Foskett. "But it's what Brian wanted, of course, and it's brilliant.

"That's how you get the term 'genius,' by having other musicians look at you and say, 'What the hell is this?' When they hear the finished product they say, 'Oh ya, I guess that does work.'"

Foskett, who has recorded and toured with several other artists in his career including Paul McCartney, Heart, Roger McGuinn, Roy Orbison, Eric Clapton, Jeff Beck, Jimmy Page, Ringo Starr, Chicago, the Moody Blues the Everly Brothers and Christopher Cross, said that these days, the myriad of problems that dogged Wilson for years — drug abuse, mental and emotional problems — are behind him.

"I think he's really healthy, both mentally and physically lately," said Foskett. "In the 1970s and 1980s, he was riddled with a lot of different troubles in his life. But when you're drug-free, alcohol-free and nicotine-free, it really frees you from a lot of those burdens.

"He could be dead, literally, by his own hand in the way that he was back then," said Foskett. "I think that releasing himself from all those things is the main thing that has put him on the track to where he is now."

And for the past several years, Wilson is enjoying his own music again because it is being played by his touring band — a band that Wilson calls the best he's ever worked with and a band called "the best touring band in the world" by McCartney — in the way that Wilson originally recorded the songs.

"With real organic instruments rather than synthesized sound," said Foskett. "And even though it takes a lot of money to put that show on the road with 11 pieces, Brian wanted a real live French horn on 'God Only Knows' and he wanted a real saxophone on 'California Girls.' If there was three guitar parts, he wanted three guitars. He really prides himself on the fact that we can present the show the way that it is."

As for returning to the Keswick Theatre, Foskett said it's become a favorite venue for Wilson and the band members.

"We like that theater. I think our agent's brother-in-law owns that theater," deadpanned Foskett. "Really, it's a great-sounding theater and the audience is always receptive. It always sells out and it's always a really fun show.

Dancing in My Underwear

"Quite a few of the band members have a lot of friends that come to th particular show for some reason," he said. "It's always a good hang for th band and Brian loves the theater."

Although I had previously interviewed Brian, it was Foskett who eventual opened the door to my meeting Brian face-to-face.

As Brian might say in the song, "Wouldn't It Be Nice," "Maybe if we thi and wish and hope and pray it might come true." And it did. I got to me Brian Wilson backstage at the Keswick Theatre.

It's not often one gets a chance to actually meet the person whose work h had such an impact on one's life.

The music has moved me, touched me and helped shape me along the wa It has helped define me as the person I am today.

But there I was, with The Blonde Accountant, backstage at the Keswic shaking hands with Brian, courtesy of Foskett.

Of course, I immediately turned into a 12-year-old boy who had ju discovered girls for the first time — sweaty, trembling hands, knees visib shaking, blathering something completely incoherent.

Brian has a nice, firm handshake. I knew he was taller than I, but he seem even a little taller than I expected. He signed a copy of my story, as d Jeffrey. I had previously purchased a 45 rpm record of "Surfer Girl" at t Rock and Roll Hall of Fame in Cleveland a few months earlier, and Bri was gracious enough to sign that as well.

I gave that signed copy of "Surfer Girl" to my daughter Kiley for h birthday the following January.

Then we had our picture taken, and Brian threw his arm around my shoulder. As an added and humbling bonus, Jeffrey mentioned that his friend Roger McGuinn — *the* Roger McGuinn, lead singer and lead guitarist on many of the Byrds' records — called Jeffrey and told him what a nice article I had written.

Wow. With apologies to The Mamas and The Papas, McGuinn and McGuire couldn't get no higher . . . and neither could I.

The whole exchange probably didn't last more than a few minutes. Those who know Brian's history know that while he is gracious with fans, he isn't particularly chatty or comfortable in meet-and-greet situations.

Still, the few moments I got to spend with him answered the question, "Wouldn't it be nice . . . to meet Brian Wilson?"

It was all of that. And so much more.

Hall & Oates
John Oates
Along with Yosemite Sam,
the go-to guy for lip hair

John Oates is just a nice guy. Flat out, plain and simple. Not only that, but he takes care of the hometown folks whenever he's in the old neighborhood.

For more than 40 years, he's been half of one of the most famous and successful duos in the history of rock and roll – Hall & Oates. But one wouldn't know it to talk to him. He's as humble and gracious as any big-name rock and roll superstar could be.

I grew up on Hall & Oates hits, many of which he co-wrote with partner Daryl Hall, including "Sara Smile," "You Make My Dreams," "She's Gone," "I Can't Go for That," "Maneater" and "Out of Touch."

I've had the opportunity to interview him a half dozen times over the years and see him up close and personal in a handful of community situations. He's performed for a students-only assembly at his alma mater, North Penn High School; he's spent time meeting people at a private reception before a solo performance at the Sellersville Theater 1894; and he's conducted a private songwriting seminar for a small group of students that was as easygoing as it was enlightening.

I was lucky enough to get invited to all those events. Not a lot of people know this, but according to Oates, he has a special bond with the Sellersville Theater 1894.

"It has a lot of significance to me," said Oates in an interview prior to a 2010 appearance there. "Back in high school, I was dating a girl from up

187

near Sellersville and we went to the movies there. I definitely go back a lor
way with the theater.

"It's a great venue acoustically and it's intimate. It's all the things I lil
when I play solo. I really like being able to be in contact with the audience
said Oates.

But it was particularly interesting to get a peek behind the curtain of tl
songwriting seminar in one of his previous visits to the area.

Oates, then fresh off a Hall & Oates performance in October 2009 at tl
Spectrum — the next-to-last group to perform at the historic venue before
closed for good at the end of that month and was eventually demolished –
was in Lansdale, Pa., for a solo gig one Saturday night at the Lansda
Center for the Performing Arts.

But several hours prior to that show, he conducted a songwriting seminar a
part of the center's "One (Wo)Man Show Series," which showcases the a
of solo performers.

The LCPA had partnered with the North Penn School District to offer a
educational experience for some of its students, and Oates, a member of tl
rock and roll wing of the Songwriters Hall of Fame, was more than happy
oblige.

The first thing he did when he walked onto the stage at the Lansdale Cent
for the Performing Arts that afternoon was make everybody feel at ease.

"I'm not going to use this," said Oates, pointing to the stool and micropho
that had been set up for him. "Let's do this."

And with that, he hopped off the stage and sat on its edge, beckoning the 3
or so people in the theater to move their chairs closer to him, which they di

"I can't teach you how to write a song," Oates told the group. "I think songwriters have a knack. Two of the keys are to learn from people who you respect and study the people who you really like."

The informal give-and-take featured not only the North Penn music students but a few seasoned musicians hoping to get some tips from somebody who has walked the walk.

Oates, who held his guitar for the entire hourlong discussion but didn't play it other than to once pluck out three simple chords to illustrate a point, stressed to the would-be songwriters to do several things — like be a well-rounded musician, keep a journal, focus on the work and not get too enamored of being famous.

"Too many kids get caught up in wanting to be famous, wanting to be known. It means absolutely nothing," he said. "Fame is a byproduct of quality and hard work."

But above all, Oates stressed that a songwriter must be true to oneself and one's emotion.

"I have expressed my deepest emotion through my songs," he said. "To me, it seems to be a natural expression of that emotion. And don't be afraid. It's the fearlessness of putting it out there in a unique and different way that will set you apart."

Oates, who lives in Colorado although his parents still resided in North Wales at the time, said he gets a lot of his ideas for songs when he's hiking or riding his bike in the mountains.

"My biggest challenge is how do I get [down the mountain] fast enough to remember it," he said.

But nowadays, Oates is more concerned with saying something really personal with his songs.

"I've written a lot of hits, but they don't mean anything to me now," he said. "For me to write a song like 'Maneater' now would be totally inappropriate. If you don't have a story to tell, you really don't have much."

Fortunately, I felt comfortable enough talking to Oates over the years to finally muster the courage to ask him in one of those interviews about one of the most unique aspects of his Hall & Oates career – the famous bushy mustache that he sported when the duo hit in big in the 1970s and 1980s.

And he invoked the name of Yosemite Sam. Yep, that Yosemite Sam - the grouchy cartoon gunslinger with the "hare-trigger" temper and archenemy of that "crazy idget galoot" Bugs Bunny.

But the only thing that John Oates and Yosemite Sam have in common is that they both have (or *have had* in Oates' case) a big bushy mustache.

As he and his music matured, Oates shaved off the mustache and moved on. But the mustache didn't. In fact, John Oates' mustache developed kind of a persona of its own and a cult following, even though it no longer had a lip on which to sit. Fans and the media perpetuated the notion.

In fact, at one point in 2009, John Oates' mustache had its own animated series called "J-Stache" on the website FunnyorDie.com. in which Oates portrayed himself while comedian Dave Attell portrayed Oates' mustache. The premise had Oates and his mustache running a celebrity health spa by day and being vigilante crimefighters by night.

"I just think it's funny," said Oates about all the hubbub surrounding his mustache and how it's taken on a life of its own. "People are always asking me about it. Just the other day, a request came in for me to sing a song for

Yosemite Sam's mustache. Just because I had one, evidently I'm now the go-to guy for anything that has to do with lip hair."

Now that's a funny quote.

Even though Oates is a good sport about it, he stressed that he has distanced himself from the mustache days.

"It represents a part of my life and the person I was back then," he said. "In a sense, the shedding of that mustache was a way for me to reinvent myself and move on with my life. I really wasn't planning on being that particular guy for the rest of my life.

"I think so many people get locked into a self-image, especially in the world of performers and show business. Their self-image becomes one and the same with them. I certainly don't feel like that particular image was me in any way and I didn't want it to be me. I always look forward to growth and not going back."

Of course, Oates was referring to personal growth and not upper lip growth. Fair enough. Still, his was one of the great stashes of all time, right up there with the likes of Salvador Dali, Albert Einstein, Hulk Hogan, Bob Goulet, Tom Selleck, Rollie Fingers and the aforementioned Yosemite Sam. (By the way, the voice of Yosemite Sam was the great Mel Blanc, who also wore a mustache, although it was more of the pencil-thin version.)

Unfortunately, I did not inherit the mustache gene from my father. My dad resembled actor Hal Linden, and with the moustache, Pop was a dead ringer for Linden's television character "Barney Miller," so much so that I would occasionally call him "Barn" in casual conversation.

I wore a mustache and goatee for seven or eight years, but the upper lip part of that equation was one of the weakest mustaches in the history of stashes.

Dancing in My Underwear

Oates' mustache would scoff at my weak entry in the stash sweepstakes. Yosemite Sam's mustache would actually berate my mustache right off my face. In fact, I believe Sam would have no trepidation at all about calling me a crazy idget galoot - that's how weak my stash was.

In hindsight, it would have been better if I had just ignored some of the more unruly nose hair and allowed it to incorporate itself into the mustache, just to add character and density to the overall effort. I believe that not doing so may have cost me my only chance for inclusion into the American Mustache Institute membership, a definite missed opportunity.

One that John Oates didn't miss.

Dan May
My album debut . . . sort of

In those moments of pure fantasy, I sometimes allow myself to think of all the cool things I'd like to do if I had an unlimited amount of disposable income.

Things like design my own home, travel the world, own a classic car or buy the Philadelphia Phillies, sit behind home plate for every home game and attempt to set the record for the highest number of hotdogs consumed in a nine-inning game.

One of the things I've always wanted to have was an area in my house — a great room — with a bunch of recliners for family and friends. I'd then hire my favorite musical groups — like the Beach Boys, Hall & Oates, America, the Doobie Brothers — and pay them whatever they wanted to come to my house for private concerts in my great room while I relax in my recliner.

It turns out that I'm not the only guy who has that fantasy. In fact, there's already something pretty close to my dream scenario for listening to music in Philadelphia.

The nonprofit Philadelphia Society for Art, Literature and Music is the brainchild of Jamey Reilly, PSALM chairman. Essentially, he and wife Suyun have turned their living room into a 60-seat entertainment venue for music, dance, comedy, performance art and literary readings, reminiscent of the old-world salons of Europe.

The Blonde Accountant and I have been there a few times and it's truly a unique experience. The intimate setting of someone's living room is a great place to watch a concert. And of course, inviting people into one's home offers the opportunity to mingle and meet the artists and the like-minded people who enjoy a particular kind of music.

The only thing that's missing at the PSALM is a big old recliner called "Mike's Chair" that I get to use when I attend shows there. I'm going to have to talk to Jamey about that. But I don't think Jamey is going to put a "Mike's Chair" in his house specifically for me. I have enough trouble getting a "Mike's Chair" designated in my own family room.

One of the artists — whom we've seen a couple of times at the PSALM — and whom we follow regularly in the Philadelphia area is Dan May.

The Blonde Accountant and I first saw Dan as the opener for country music star Crystal Gayle at the Sellersville Theater 1894 in December 2007.

It was another one of those "hey, this guy is pretty good" moments for us. We purchased a CD from Dan after the show and we've been "Dan Fans" ever since, traveling throughout the Philadelphia region for years to watch him perform at various venues.

Dan is not only a talented singer and songwriter, but he's also an interesting and genuinely nice guy. And he has quite a resume — ice cream truck driver, worker making gear-shift covers in a rubber factory, track coach, nuclear missile security guard and gravedigger among others.

Oh, and he was an opera singer . . . quite by accident.

"Most of those jobs happened between the time I got out of high school and college," said May, originally from Sandusky, Ohio. "For the gravedigging job, you just have to be able to handle a shovel. Nothing like a constant reminder of your mortality at age 18, when you're feeling most immortal."

194

In addition to Crystal Gayle, May has opened for Suzy Bogguss, Hal Ketchum and B.J. Thomas, all at the Sellersville Theater 1894. He has also performed at the Tin Angel in Philadelphia, Milkboy coffeehouse in Ardmore and Chaplin's in Spring City as well as at Musikfest in Bensalem, Pa.

For the past several years, May has been pursuing a career in popular music.

"It was totally by mistake. I was going to school for journalism. I wanted to be a newspaper writer," said May.

He decided that journalism wasn't for him, transferred from Bowling Green University to Ohio State University and started all over, pursuing a different career path.

"I had no musical training at all. And the dean at the music school said, 'I don't think you should even bother doing this,'" he said.

But May threw caution to the wind and got into the college's music composition program anyway.

"I was in my first year and somebody heard me sing and said, 'You know, your voice would be ideal for opera.' I'd never been to an opera, never sung any classical music. I gave it a try and I liked it," he said.

So after one more semester, May switched to a vocal performance major and was accepted to the highly competitive performance division. After earning his degree, he then got a four-year scholarship to the Academy of Vocal Arts in Philadelphia.

That led to a professional opera singing career that lasted 15 years and allowed him to perform across the United States and Canada, a career that was then cut short by a vocal cord problem that required surgery and limited the range and amplification needed for May to sing opera.

He dabbled in opera directing and spent three years in a ballet production, but his interest in songwriting and popular music had been rekindled.

"I had turned off that part of my brain for 15 years, that creative part," said May. "For me, singing opera was never genuine emotion, and maybe that's why I never felt like I was at home singing opera.

"I'm at my best when I'm singing my music. I think it's because I enjoy creating. In opera, you're more duplicating. Singing words and music that have been around for hundreds of years, you have an opportunity to make it your own, but it never felt like it was my own," he said. "I think that sort of music shut off my creativity."

May said that writing provides him an outlet for his creativity and the performing offers him positive feedback from the audience.

"Performing takes it to another level. There is an energy you can feed off of and it's always fun to hear people in the audience singing a song that you wrote by yourself in your living room," he said. "I take a lot of pride in the words."

May said the response to his music has been "amazing."

"Because of the Internet, I'm able to reach a larger audience than I would have been able to 10 years ago."

His first two CDs, "Once Was Red" and "Fate Said Nevermind," have been described as having "unforgettable melodies, layered harmonies and engaging lyrics." His third CD, "The Long Road Home," was recorded

Morning Star Studios in Spring House, Pennsylvania, just a few miles from where my office is at Montgomery Media.

"I think people who are familiar with my first two CDs will see a marked difference in the quality of sound in the third CD. And I hope that I'm always evolving as a songwriter," said May.

And evolve he did. Dan's fourth CD, "Dying Breed," released in May 2011, featured the song "Paradise," which turns out to be something a little different from what the title suggests.

The lyrics of the song feature things like America's addiction to corn syrup, the manipulation practiced by pharmaceutical companies, global warming, plastic surgery, the use of the attention-deficit hyperactivity disorder-treating drug Ritalin and swipes at Fox News, Facebook, the banking industry and bailout and even the Catholic Church.

Some description of paradise, huh?

"There's a real connecting thread from song to song," said May. "It's a look back at the good old days that maybe weren't as good as we thought they were."

Dan is an Americana-folk-tinged troubadour whose soft voice and thought-provoking lyrics have made him one of my all-time favorite artists.

And I really liked the CD "Dying Breed," not only because I thought it was his best work to date, but because it was the album on which I made my debut.

No, I didn't do any singing or playing of the instruments. That would be silly since I don't sing or play an instrument. And no, I didn't contribute to the writing of any of the lyrics. Dan wouldn't be able to sell any CDs if I would have been involved in any of that.

But it was the first CD that actually had my name on it, in the "thank you" section, with seventh billing. Apparently I have written a few stories over the years about Dan that he liked and he wanted to appropriately acknowledge that.

I didn't know he was going to include my name on the CD until I got it and looked at the small type. Dan didn't tell me ahead of time. And it was quite a pleasant surprise.

So I decided to write a chapter in this book about him and tell the rest of the world how much I like his music.

And I didn't tell him about it ahead of time.

The Lovin' Spoonful
Joe Butler
I believe in backstage magic

Put together a guy who asks questions for a living with a guy who likes to tell stories and it's pretty easy to kill an hour.

The difference this time was the guy doing the talking – Joe Butler of the Lovin' Spoonful – and the stories he was sharing were about making music in the 1960s and included names like Brian Wilson, Ed Sullivan and legendary record producer Phil Spector.

That makes it a really unique and special way to kill an hour.

That's just what happened Friday night at the Sellersville Theater 1894 between two performances by the Lovin' Spoonful in the summer of 2011.

The band – whose original members included two rockers from Long Island, Butler and Steve Boone, who got together with two folk musicians from Greenwich Village, John Sebastian and Zal Yanovsky – hit it big in the mid-to-late 1960s with hits like "Do You Believe in Magic," "Daydream," "You Didn't Have to be So Nice," "Nashville Cats" and "Summer in the City."

I had interviewed Butler to preview the shows. He admitted that today's version of the Lovin' Spoonful doesn't rely on past glories from what he called its 15 minutes of fame in the 1960s.

"But we deliver the goods. I'm pretty clumsy at drawing a picture but Jerry [Yester] and I can sing anything now. The group is strong," said Butler.
The Lovin' Spoonful carved a niche for itself — right in the middle of the "British Invasion." Back then, Sebastian carried most of the lead vocals, along with drummer-vocalist Butler, bassist Boone and guitarist Yanovsky.

199

Dancing in My Underwear

The songs endured, the group changed and evolved and eventually wei inducted to both the Rock and Roll Hall of Fame and Vocal Group Hall c Fame.

"We had three lead singers then. It was like the Marx Brothers witho Zeppo," said Butler. "Zally's contribution as a guitarist is staggering. F could play any style; it was just natural to him."

"Some of those songs I thought would really last," said Butler in a telephoi interview from his home in the Berkshires. "Like a good play, it was a goc story, a good melody line, good singing, well-performed — I listen to tl songs from back then and think, 'Oh, I was playing pretty kick-ass.'"

Although music has been his life — he said he was bitten by the music the 1950s while listening to the early rockabilly of Elvis Presley — Butl spent some time as a thespian, and credits some of his singing longevity the late Broadway and "Law and Order" star Jerry Orbach.

"I learned some very good voice tricks from him," said Butler, who h stepped out from behind the drums and handles a majority of the lead voca now. "He said first of all, it's breathing. You don't lose your voice whe performing; it's after the show. Don't go out to a restaurant or nightclu where there is noise to talk over. You've got to shut up for a while, gi\ everything a rest and calm down. You had your hour to strut on stage. No you're off the stage. Take all the ego out and join the human race."

Sebastian left the group to pursue a solo career in 1968. Yanovsky had left year earlier (he died in 2002) and was replaced by Yester. The original fo last performed together in a 1979 show in the Catskills.

Butler, who turned 70 in 2011 — his daughter is actress Yancy Butler of tl TV series "Man and Machine" and "South Beach" and films "Hard Targe and "Drop Zone" — said the music and the group have endured because some of those early hits were life-affirming songs.

"There was no dark side to the music, so it was embraced," he said. "Also, in our day, there was a thing called a variety show, where families sat and watched something together. We were perfect for that. The songs that are endearing are the ones that have compassion, understanding and enlightenment and are fun."

Although there are pockets of original fans who remember and still enjoy the Lovin' Spoonful sound, the music — like all good music — has transcended generations.

"Because of extended air play, there are people who are much younger who know our music, so we do have a cross-generational crowd," said Butler. "It depends on if we play at a park or an amusement park where there are a lot of kids, and a lot of them know our stuff. Their parents have played it for them."

Butler said at the time he was looking forward to playing at a venue like the Sellersville Theater 1894.

"I did a lot of acting, so these types of theaters are my favorites. I feel like I'm on hallowed ground," he said. "We play all the hits, which everybody wants to hear. People will recognize those songs. It's just like if they were going to a barbecue and we were the neighbors' kids on the porch playing music for them."

"It's a privilege and honor to share the songs. It really is. It means the world to every one of us."

It was a fun interview, and on the night of the performance, The Blonde Accountant and I got to go into the green room and meet Butler and other

Dancing in My Underwear

band members, including Yester, who played piano on "Do You Believe
Magic" in 1965 and joined the band full-time in 1967.

Butler and Yester – the brother of Jim Yester of another '60s group, t
Association – are just two happy and friendly guys who have been makir
music for more than 40 years. We sat there and listened as they told sto
after story about their musical journeys. Butler talked about meeting F
Sullivan for the first time. Yester talked about being in an adjoining stud
when Brian Wilson was recording the famous "Pet Sounds" album.

Of course, it was the '60s and these guys were young rock-and-rollers,
there were some, uh . . . illicit substance references sprinkled here and the
into some of the stories.

The only band member we didn't get to meet was Steve Boone, one of t
original four, who Butler said was taking a nap between shows. Hey, the
guys aren't spring chickens anymore so old-guy jokes appeared to be fa
game as well.

At one point, Butler looked at me and said, "I better quit talking, I'
starting to get hoarse." And then he proceeded to tell stories for another ha
hour.

Butler, Yester and I even goofed around for a photo before we exited tl
green room. Yester is giving me the bunny ears in the picture. My kind
guys, those two were that evening.

It was a fascinating and entertaining experience – oh, and the show w
great, too – and I appreciated having had the opportunity to get a look
artists that most fans don't get a chance to experience.

Hey, I believe in magic.

The Four Seasons
Bob Gaudio
Hey, get your hind end out of my ear, pal!

At this age, in my fifties, birthdays aren't such a big deal. My dad was that way. At some point, I guess when he was around 70 or so, he never cared whether he got gifts for his birthday or at Christmas.

For reasons that I didn't understand then, his attitude puzzled me. I'd say, "Dad, what do you want for your birthday?" And he'd answer, "Nothing. I just want to be with my family."

As my daughters got older and began to develop their own lives – aspects of which increasingly didn't include their old man – I had a better appreciation for what my dad was saying. Material things like gifts didn't matter.

So for the past several years, that's been my approach as well, which frustrates the gift-givers in my life. I'm very difficult to buy for because all I want is to be with my family.

But that didn't deter The Blonde Accountant when it came time to getting me something for my 52nd birthday in 2011. She is very good in these types of situations. Mostly what she's very good at is knowing her husband.

And I was quite surprised and pleased when I opened my birthday card to find dinner reservations for the Capital Grille in Philadelphia, followed by tickets to see "Jersey Boys" at the historic Forrest Theatre in the city's theater district.

The Capital Grille is one of those "big date night" restaurants that we prefer for special occasions. The New York Times has written that "The national reputation of The Capital Grille has crowds beating down the doors." And it's true. One has to make reservations several weeks in advance to get table.

It's a big steak kind of joint. And over the years, I learned that one doesr go to a big-time steak place and order seafood. Give me the biggest steak the house, the Fred Flintstone cut, the one that hangs over all sides of tl plate.

For this birthday, that was the 24 oz. porterhouse steak. One can never g wrong ordering a steak as big as one's head.

The Blonde Accountant opted for the 8 oz. filet. She is a dainty girlie-g eater and has absolutely no use for a steak as big as my head. We had couple of glasses of wine, I made some googly eyes at her, and the evenir got off to a romantic start. Good food and good wine will do that.

Since it was late December, there was a chill in the air. The theater w about a six-block walk from the restaurant, but it wasn't too cold to mal the trek. Had it been a touch warmer, a casual six-block stroll, with her ar in mine, would have only added that much more to what was shaping up be a memorable birthday.

We arrived at the Forrest Theatre about 45 minutes ahead of the 8 p.r curtain. The theater, built in 1927 by the Shubert organization, is one of tl city's premiere venues for live theater. Over the years, it has presented son of the best Broadway touring productions, including "Mamma Mia!" "Tl Phantom of the Opera," "Les Miserables" and "Avenue Q."

The Blonde Accountant had been there once before, but it was my first tin in the theater. Its ornate interior architecture is impressive, but it didn't tal me long to realize that something was amiss and that it was going to be difficult evening for my back, hips and knees.

Tickets to "Jersey Boys" are not inexpensive. The Blonde Accountant paid $136.50 for each ticket. My seat at the ballpark costs only $26. It didn't take me long to realize that the other advantage my seat at the ballpark affords me is that it actually has enough room for my hind end. This is not the case with the seats at the Forrest Theatre.

Our seats were in the third row in the mezzanine, which offers a great view of the stage, assuming one can squeeze into the chairs. But that wasn't all. Not only are the seats not wide enough, but they're not deep enough either. Only when I got my backside wedged into the seat did I realize that my knees were in the back of the ears of the lady in the seat in front of me. I'm sure that was a pleasant experience for her, one that likely wasn't spelled out in a disclaimer on the back of her $136.50 ticket.

Now I am not opposed to snuggling up to The Blonde Accountant when tight quarters force the issue. In fact, I quite like it.

But I am opposed to having some other guy sitting in my lap when I'm already trying to sit there, which is what happened when the seatmate to my right entered our row and prepared to sit down. It was such a tight squeeze that when he tried to remove his coat before he sat down, his tush was in my ear. Hey, at least I had the common courtesy to give the lady in front of me my knees and not my tush.

So for the final 20 minutes before the show started, I was scouring the Playbill for contact information for Forrest Theatre honchos, intent on sending whoever that was a scathing email expressing my displeasure at having my wife pay $136.50 for some stranger to put his butt in my ear.

Then the show started. And this is how good "Jersey Boys" is: By the end of the two-and-a-half hour performance, I had completely forgotten about my aching knees and my neighbor's rear end.

Dancing in My Underwear

"Jersey Boys" is a documentary musical about the Four Seasons – wi
original members Frankie Valli, Bob Gaudio, Tommy DeVito and Ni
Massi – one of the most successful rock and roll groups of the 1960s. It fi
opened on Broadway in 2005, won the 2006 Tony Award for best music
and has had two national tours since. The show we saw was part of th
second national tour, which included a five-week run in Philadelphia.

I grew up with the Four Seasons, listening to such No. 1 hits as "Sherry
"Big Girls Don't Cry," "Walk Like a Man," "Rag Doll" and "Decemb
1963 (Oh What a Night)." Later, when lead singer Frankie Valli was a so
act, his music was often found on my eight-track and cassette players.

"Jersey Boys" is an absolutely fabulous show. Not only are the music a
the acting stellar, but the story of the history of The Four Seasons a
Frankie Valli himself is compelling.

After the show, The Blonde Accountant and I walked the six blocks back
the Capital Grille where we had left our car in the valet parking lot. It turn
out to be a very special birthday for me, despite the challenges presented I
the Forrest Theatre seats. It occurred to me that my wife and I had just ma
another one of those special memories for ourselves, and the music
Frankie Valli and the Four Seasons had played a major role in helping mal
that happen.

Five days later, I was on the phone with Bob Gaudio - one of the origin
Four Seasons and the guy who wrote many of those wonderful hits for tl
group – for an interview about the Philly run of "Jersey Boys."

Hey Bob, you're a Jersey boy who's got a lot of stroke in Philly, anythi
you can do about those pain-in-butt seats in the mezzanine at the Forr
Theatre?

"You know something, this is not the first time I've heard about this with these old, beautiful theaters," said Gaudio. "They're so gorgeous when you look at them. And it's the same way with the theaters we've played in London, and oddly enough, in Melbourne and Sydney [Australia].

"They're just wonderful, they sound fantastic, but they all have the same problem and there's only one solution – take out some seats. I've fought this battle time and time again and there's not a whole lot I can do."

Well, at least he didn't think it was a stupid question.

It was interesting to talk to one of the original Four Seasons so soon after seeing "Jersey Boys." The story that's presented onstage answers a lot of the questions about the group's journey and its music. Still, it's cool to actually hear it directly from one of the guys who lived it.

Like the famous handshake deal that Gaudio and Frankie Valli have had that has been the cornerstone of an even 50-50 split partnership that has lasted nearly 50 years.

"It works. I've often said that maybe if we put it on paper, it won't work anymore," said Gaudio. "No matter what's on paper, you still have to live up to what you think the intent of that document was. So it's really what you feel in your heart and what you think the deal is. So why not a handshake?"

Gaudio said that he and Valli have been like brothers, with all the ups and downs that come with such a relationship.

"But when the time comes, we're still in each other's corner," he said. "We don't travel together, we don't do the same things; we haven't for years. He's on the road and he does what he does and I do what I do; I produce and I'm behind the scenes."

Dancing in My Underwear

Gaudio added that he and Valli still offer advice to each other on occasion but stresses that the two control their own destinies and live in their own separate worlds.

"It comes down to respect for each other's talent and what the other guy's vision is and giving someone enough room to breathe – like a marriage," said Gaudio.

One of my favorite aspects of the Four Seasons' story is the fact that it intersected in the early years with actor Joe Pesci, who won the Academy Award for Best Supporting Actor for his role as mobster Tommy DeVito in the 1990 film "Goodfellas," which is one of my favorite movies of all-time.

It was Pesci, another real-life Jersey boy, who introduced Gaudio to Valli and the other band members back in the early 1960s and that introduction and subsequent partnership catapulted the Four Seasons into stardom.

"Joe and I grew up together and played in a jazz band, as noted in 'Jersey Boys,'" said Gaudio. "We had a jazz quartet for about a year, a year-and-a half and essentially starved to death. We decided then it was time to go our separate ways."

But that early bond between childhood friends was never broken. When Pesci got the role in the Martin Scorsese film "Goodfellas," nearly 30 years after he and Gaudio parted musically, the name of the character Pesci played was "Tommy DeVito" – taken from his friend of the same name, Tommy DeVito who played guitar for the original Four Seasons.

How cool is that?

And that's how my 52nd birthday ended up being a memorable one. I spent wonderful evening with The Blonde Accountant, we saw the fabulous stage production of "Jersey Boys" and then less than a week later, I got to talk to Bob Gaudio, one of the original Jersey boys.

It seems appropriate to give the last word in this instance to Frankie Valli, as written for him by Bob Gaudio . . . "Oh what a night."

Epilogue
Elton John
I guess that's why they call it the blues

The first time that writing and music intersected for me was at Pekin Community High School in 1976. That's where I was first introduced to Mrs. Betty Bower's journalism class, and I liked it so much that I immediately knew that I wanted to be a newspaperman, a deep conviction that never left me and eventually led to a 36-year career in the newsroom.

Not only did I discover that I liked to write – which was lucky for me because I was somewhere between extremely mediocre to downright terrible in just about every other subject except lunch – but I had a very cool teaching assistant from nearby Bradley University in Peoria for that journalism class.

George Jasinski – we affectionately called him "Mr. J." – was in his final year of college, majoring in journalism, and was completing his student teaching requirement by spending the semester with us in Mrs. Bower's journalism class, where one of his main responsibilities was advising us on producing the school newspaper.

Mr. J. was only 5 years older than we were, but he was the epitome of cool. When I tell people in the Philadelphia area now that I'm originally from Illinois, the first thing they usually say is, "Oh, you're from Chicago."

Well, no, not really. I'm from three hours south of Chicago. And what people not from Illinois don't understand is that in my home state, there is Chicago and then there is everyplace else in the state that's *not* Chicago, and most of the rest of it is located in or near Hicksville, U.S.A.

211

Dancing in My Underwear

Mr. J. was a Chicago native, which made him Chicago cool to the 16-year-old budding journalists who grew up in the relatively rural existence of central Illinois.

Here's how cool Mr. J. was: One day after school – and this was after we had done our work and put the latest issue of the Pekinois, the school newspaper, to bed – Mr. J. taught me and Mikki Milam, one of our school's cheerleaders whom I had a crush on but was never able to tell her, how to do the "Hustle."

The "Hustle" was a dance – remember, it was 1976 and disco music was just making its presence known in the cornfields of central Illinois – and Mr. J was quite the dancer . . . at least Mikki and I thought he was.

So we moved some of the desks out of the way and Mr. J. spent some time teaching Mikki and me how to do the "Hustle," right there in Mrs. Bower' classroom.

Although my dancing skills were never more than questionable at best despite all the effort put forth by Mr. J. in those early years to teach me few steps, he and I did develop a friendship. He was, after all, the one who encouraged me to pursue journalism as a career, even though he gave it up relatively quickly after graduating from college and went on to be successful attorney in the Chicago area.

But after the school year was over, Mr. J. went back to Chicago in th summer of 1976 and I went about the business of playing summer baseba because even though I had found some direction toward a career i journalism, I still wanted to become a professional baseball player at th point.

It was about this time that I discovered the music of Elton John. My sist Casey, who was three years my junior, was a big Elton John fan and m folks had gotten her what was Elton's ninth studio album "Captain Fantastic and the Brown Dirt Cowboy." The album was released in 1975 and debuted at No. 1 on the pop album charts. The only single to make it big from the album was "Someone Saved My Life Tonight," which topped out at No. 4 that year on the singles chart.

By the summer of 1976, Elton John had a pretty big presence among the teenagers in our household, and when Elton's summer tour schedule revealed that he was doing a show in Chicago, my sister and I were both in my dad's ear about driving us the three hours north to see the concert.

Fortunately, we knew a guy in Chicago – the very cool Mr. J. – whom we thought could hook us up with tickets. So when my dad green-lighted the road trip if I could secure some seats to the concert, I reached out to Mr. J.

Of course, he was so Chicago cool and connected in his city that tickets to the show were no problem. The plan was that my dad would drive my sister and me to Chicago, where we would hook up with Mr. J. and his sister and all go see Elton John perform at the International Amphitheatre, at Halstead and 42nd streets in Chicago, adjacent to the famous Union Stock Yards, the meatpacking district in Chicago for more than a century.

The landmark Amphitheatre seated approximately 9,000 people and at that time was only about eight years removed from being the site of the 1968 Democratic National Convention, which featured anti-Vietnam War protesting and rioting that made it one of the most tumultuous political conventions in American history. The venue was eventually demolished in 1999.

Certainly we didn't know it at the time, but we were going to see what would become one of the most legendary performers in the history of pop music in what would be considered a legendary and historic auditorium in the city of Chicago. Man, I wish I still had the ticket stub from that concert.

Dancing in My Underwear

Of course, Elton was at his freaky best in the mid-1970s, especially with his wardrobe, which for its time out-Liberaced even the great Liberace for sheer flamboyance. Our seats were on the floor of the theater, in the back, about as far away from the stage as we could be.

My sister – who at age 13 was convinced that she was someday going to marry Elton John – recalls that we rushed the stage at some point, but the one memory I have of that show is my dad standing on a folding chair in the back of the Amphitheatre, rocking out with the rest of the kids to Elton's music. I never asked him about it, but my sister and I are convinced that he was a then-50-year-old Elton John fan, which would have been consistent with my parents' relative hipness when it came to popular music over the course of several decades.

The next time I saw Elton John was five years later in 1981, while I was a student at the University of Iowa. Elton was performing at Hilton Coliseum on the campus of Iowa State University in Ames, which is about a two-hour drive from Iowa City. I was familiar with the venue because I had spent the first two years of my college career at Iowa State University and had been in Hilton Coliseum many times for college basketball games and wrestling matches.

Once again, my sister – who was still not married to Elton at that point – went along with me and a couple of other guys I knew from Iowa City. Once again we were about as far away from the stage as we could be, all the way in the back of the auditorium. This time we were in the nosebleed seats, not on the floor, so there was no need to stand on our chairs.

That Elton John concert experience was mostly uneventful, but I was well into the college experience at the time and the youthful exuberance of partying that usually accompanied a concert in the early 1980s may be responsible for the lack of additional details that I can recall surrounding that event.

The next time I saw Elton John was around 1992 and I was married, with a toddler. We were living in Springfield, Illinois, at the time, and Elton was appearing once again in Ames, Iowa - only this time he was performing at Jack Trice Stadium, where the Iowa State Cyclones played football. That place seats more than 50,000, and tickets were being sold through Ticketmaster, going on sale on a Saturday morning.

The plan was this: Rather than call Iowa and try to order tickets over the phone where interest was likely to be high, I decided to go down to the box office at the Prairie Capital Convention Center in Springfield, where I was pretty convinced there wouldn't be a line for the Elton John concert in Ames, Iowa. That way, I could easily order tickets for the show through Ticketmaster without waiting in line.

I was correct. There wasn't a line at the Prairie Capital Convention Center. I went right up to the box office and ordered two tickets, at $75 each, right on the 25-yard line, as close to the stage as I had ever been for an Elton John concert. The plan had worked to perfection.

Almost. But I wouldn't know it until we actually got to the concert. As it turned out, the seats – folding chairs placed on the playing area of the football field – were on the 25-yard-line, but it was the wrong 25-yard line. We were actually at the other end of the field, 75 yards from the stage.

When Elton came onstage, all of the people in the folding chairs on the field stood up, and we couldn't see a thing. This did not sit well with my first wife, Sherry, especially for what was considered a pretty steep ticket price at the time.

But it was Elton John and we did what everybody else did in that situation: We stood on our folding chairs to get a better look at the stage. Everybody, and I mean everybody, scheduled to sit in folding chairs in that stadium that day for that concert was in fact standing on those chairs.

215

Dancing in My Underwear

After surveying the thousands of people standing on folding chairs for the first of Elton's songs, a guard working security for the concert decided he was going to exercise his authority. And the two people he picked out of that huge crowd to tell to get down off the folding chairs were me and my wife.

Now I have a policy of never messing with authority figures who have the ability to throw my behind in jail. Nothing good can come of that.

My first wife, well, she didn't practice that same approach, especially at those prices. In all fairness, she had a point in this particular situation: There were 10,000 people standing on folding chairs trying to get a better look at Elton John. The security guard was not asking any of those others to get down off their chairs, just her and I.

I complied. She did not. It wasn't more than a few minutes before the guard came back over, tapped her on the leg, and once again asked her to get down off the chair. It was loud, but I believe she suggested to him that he go do something to himself that I'm pretty sure was physically impossible.

It was at this point that I reached into my front pocket to check and see how much cash I had in hand, thinking that I was going to need bail money to get my wife out of jail.

Fortunately for all involved, the fans on the field calmed down after Elton's first couple of songs and we settled into our seats. Although we were up and down for most of that concert, we were no longer bothered by any security and I saved $200 in bail money.

The most recent time I've seen Elton John was in August of 2009. He was appearing with Billy Joel at Citizens Bank Ballpark in Philadelphia. That show marked the fourth decade in which I would see Elton perform.

As is the custom with me attending Elton John concerts, I once again had tickets about as far away from the stage as I could be, this time in the upper deck of the ballpark down the first-base line. Some of the differences this time included having a different wife – The Blonde Accountant was with me for this concert - not having to stand on a folding chair to see everything, and not having to worry about being bothered by overzealous security people, which in turn meant that I didn't have to worry about having enough bail money.

Once again, Elton put on a good show, and The Blonde Accountant and I danced in the nether regions of the ballpark to "Crocodile Rock," which I had now heard Elton sing live in the 1970s, the 1980s, the 1990s and now the 2000s.

And more than 35 years later . . . I still haven't been able to score an interview with Elton John. Unlike most of the rest of the soundtrack of my life that I have talked to, an interview with Elton has continued to elude me.

To be fortunate enough to have talked to Brian Wilson of the Beach Boys, Olivia Newton-John, Barry Manilow, Micky Dolenz of the Monkees, Tommy Chong and all the rest who made up the soundtrack of my life has been a remarkable run of good fortune. I am grateful that my job has provided me with those opportunities.

But it's disappointing that an interview with Elton John continues to be the one that got away, or more accurately, the one that never has been up to this point.

Maybe the next best thing – and the one aspect that could bring the soundtrack of my life full circle – might be to get out an Elton John CD, pop it in the CD player . . . and dance around in my underwear.

Yes, I remember when rock was young. And man, I've had so much fun.

Dancing in My Underwear

Acknowledgements

The special times in life are always more special for me when I can share them with the people I love. To the love of my life, my wife Judy – The Blonde Accountant – I couldn't have done this without you. Your love and encouragement inspired me and I'm so thankful we got to share many of these memories. Thanks for having faith in me and loving me no matter what happens.

To my daughters Kiley and Lexi, you, too, lived some of these memories. You both have grown up to be wonderful young women and I am so very proud of you both. This project was always about getting something on the record for you and future generations of our family.

To my stepchildren, Kaitie and Kevin, I've watched you grow and I've always appreciated that you unconditionally accepted me into your lives. Your mom is special to me, and so are you both.

Several other people also helped this project become a reality, including my mother, Ann Morsch, and my sister, Casey Gambetti, who helped me recall details from my early years, and my brother Matt Morsch, who is always there for me; and to childhood and now lifelong friends Greg Batton, Gary Psinas and Dan Brewington, who filled in some of the gaps in my memory when it came to remembering our teenage shenanigans.

Thanks to my former boss, Betsy Wilson, who always had faith in both me and my writing and for sticking by me through the difficult times; to my friend Reg Henry, deputy editorial page editor at the Pittsburgh Post-Gazette, who has been my mentor for years and because of that, I have become a better writer; to Michael Pladus, superintendent of Upper Dublin School District, a trusted advisor and huge music fan, for his words of wisdom and encouragement; to Ted Taylor, mentor, friend, writer and a great baseball guy; and to Montgomery Media and its parent company,

Journal Register Company, which offered the opportunity to have a job that afforded me the chance to meet and write about interesting people.

The two venues mentioned most often in this book – the Sellersville Theater 1894 and the Keswick Theatre – always took care of me when it came to getting access to the artists. Special thanks go to Sellersville Theater 1894 owner William Quigley and Keswick Theatre manager Judith Herbst and their wonderful staffs for the kindness, courtesy and professionalism.

Agent Jonathan Wolfson always made sure I had access to Philadelphia music icons Daryl Hall and John Oates; Jean Sievers never failed to hook me up with any of the Beach Boys; J. Patrice Kaluza – executive director of Sea Sound Studio Entertainment – paved the way for me to talk with Ken Delo of the Lawrence Welk Show; and Rosa Navarro-Hoffman was kind enough to set up an interview with original "Hawaii Five-0" star Al Harrington.

And finally, my editor, Frank Quattrone, was an invaluable friend and mentor throughout this project. His expertise in editing and his endless encouragement and enthusiasm for my story were so much more than could have expected. Without him, this book simply would not have been possible.